George Burnham

Secrets in fowl breeding

George Burnham

Secrets in fowl breeding

ISBN/EAN: 9783337146641

Printed in Europe, USA, Canada, Australia, Japan

Cover: Foto ©Lupo / pixelio.de

More available books at **www.hansebooks.com**

PART TWO. FIFTH EDITION.

SECRETS

IN

FOWL BREEDING.

By GEO. P. BURNHAM.

A COMPANION TREATISE TO

"DISEASES OF DOMESTIC POULTRY."

PRICE, FIFTY CENTS.

MELROSE, MASS.

1877.

AMERICAN LIGHT BRAHMA COCK AND PULLET. Bred by G. P. Burnam, Melrose, Mass.

PREFACE. (PART TWO.)

THE present treatise, in form and size like its predecessor in the series, will be found devoted to explanations of some of the prominent SECRETS *in fowl breeding* which are not usually familiar to fanciers.

Like the contents of my late previous work on " Poultry Diseases," this book is couched in plain language, and no attempt is made at a display of superior knowledge upon the points treated herein. Whatever is detailed, is set down as the results of practical personal experience. A demonstrated fact is worth a thousand theories.

Attention is called to the well executed frontispiece of' this book. There may be counted some sixty specimens, of over twenty-five varieties of " MODERN TENANTS OF THE AMERICAN POULTRY-YARD," combined in this picture; photographed, or drawn and engraved for us, from the best *standard* domestic fowls in the United States. And these delineations are accurate representations of all the prominent kinds of poultry now generally bred in this country — from the stalwart Light and Dark Brahmas or Cochins, to the diminutive Seabrights and Game Bantams, now popular among us.

The improvement of domestic live stock of all descriptions (poultry included), observes S. L. Goodale in his " Principles of Breeding," so as greatly to enhance their individual and aggregate value, and to render the rearing of them more profitable to all concerned, is one of the achievements of advanced civilization and enlightenment; and is as much a triumph of science and skill, as is the construction of a railway, a steamship, a telegraph, or any grand work of architecture.

Theories are promulgated, opinions are paraded before the public eye, and vast numbers of books are issued, giving us light occasionally upon many intricate points that have confused the ordinary mind through their natural but hitherto unaccounted-for ramifications.

We know the fresh green blades of grass rise in the spring from the old rootlet that has been frozen solid six months in the previous winter's earth. Can we tell *why* — except on generally accepted principles? Or can we answer why the beautiful flower is produced, in due season, from the ugly little seed we deposit in the ground?

How much less can we know (with all our study, arguments, and theories) how and why the almost invisible globular germ lying dormant within the egg-sack of a bird, may through Nature's inexplicable laws ripen to the hard-shelled egg; from which, through subsequent still more mysterious " incubation," comes forth the perfect living chick, in course of time?

The reader is referred to the following pages for some interesting facts regarding these SECRETS — wrought out through actual and repeated experiment by   THE AUTHOR.

Melrose, Mass., 1877.

SECRETS IN FOWL BREEDING.

PART TWO.

SELECTING AND MATING POULTRY STOCK.

ONE of the first secrets to be acquired by the ambitious fowl-keeper, is embodied in the title-line which heads this chapter. A consideration of primal consequence towards the successful reproduction of first-class improved domestic poultry is a proper and fortunate *selection* of the breeding stock, of whatever variety we may elect to experiment with. And this should be obtained from a reliable source, out of a well established "strain" of its class.

An important secret in fowl-breeding is to ascertain, before commencing operations, if the birds the fancier may prefer to *variety*, are the best bred or the purest-blooded to be , of their distinctive sort. It is idle to attempt to breed good chickens from poor specimens, or from imperfect stock; no matter what the *kind* of fowl may be that is chosen to begin with.

The taste of breeders differs widely among different men as to the class of fowls to which they give preference. And although the majority of poulterers now-a-days incline to favor the larger breeds, — as the Brahmas, the various colored Cochins, etc., — there are hundreds who prefer the Houdans, the Dorkings, the White and Brown Leghorns, the Black Spanish, the Polands, the Games, the Plymouth Rocks, the Dominiques, the Crested fowls, or even the beautiful little Bantams, as their choice.

But each and all of these varieties are now so largely disseminated over this country, that there is little difficulty in obtaining *any* desired kind, at moderate cost; it being necessary only to make sure that what is purchased be had from a source where the chosen birds have been carefully and honestly bred, as nearly as may be in their purity.

We must not expect to obtain for our purposes *absolutely* pure-bred domestic fowls, however. There is no such thing. Yet the different notable "strains" of different varieties now produced in American yards are good enough.

The several importations made by our breeders from China and England in the last thirty years have come to be a good deal "mixed," from time to time, on this side of the Atlantic; and it is now necessary to procure your fancy breeding stock of the *best* Americanized strains you can obtain.

Among these established strains, as we have just hinted, there are many that are choice in quality, and as good as, or better, than the best ever imported from abroad; rendered so through careful home cultivation among us.

This point being satisfactorily determined, we should next enquire in advance if the specimens to be bought are nearly related — say brother and sisters. If the chicks chosen are from eggs laid by different *hens* of the same kind — though bred to the same cock — it is as well; provided the birds are nicely pointed, thrifty, and of good standard color.

But the more distant the actual relationship is, the better; since the progeny from birds bred too closely, in this respect, rarely prove so satisfactory as those obtained from stock (of both sexes) *not* nearly allied in kin.

A chief secret in the production of the most uniformly good chicks, from any parentage, lies in securing a reliable *sire*, and in breeding such a two-year old male bird upon one-year old pullets. Two-year old fowls of *both* sexes bred together, give us very good younglings. But I have found that vigorous twelve months old pullets, bred to a good cock in his full second year, will throw better chickens on the average than others — all things else being equal.

In choosing your sire, it should be done with a view to reproducing his superior form, stamina, and color — whatever these may be — in the variety selected. The cock must possess *these* indicated qualities, in full vigor and beauty. Such male bird should be a good one, and he should be known to come from a reliable bird, like himself.

If you breed the progeny thus obtained back to the *old* bird, you are pretty sure to retain the better qualities of your strain by the means, and are quite certain that you will get the general color and symmetry of your first choice.

For your hens, look for good layers, of generous size, color even and pure, of stout constitution and symmetrical form. From among their product select the best pointed and most perfect in general characteristics, for future breeding, and you will be largely successful, as a rule, in the end.

The first one or two litters of eggs laid by pullets are not so serviceable, so sure, or so profitable for hatching, as are their later product. The eggs of two-year old hens, bred to a one-year old cock, have proved very generally successful in my experience. I am quite satisfied, however, that the most reliable breeding-birds that can be mated together, as to age, are those of one sex or the other that are a year the oldest. Two-year old birds, of any variety, are deemed at their best age — by our most experienced breeders.

The cock should be changed every spring from one clutch of pullets to another. For fine breeding, the same cock should be bred to the same run of hens but for a single season. This is an excellent plan, and those who have not tried it, will learn its advantages through experience.

Two cocks, in breeding-time, should never be kept with your hens in the same enclosure, whatever their age or their variety. The frequent contentious attention of two males to the hens, or pullets (even if the cocks do not quarrel with each other), not only annoys the females, but it absolutely injures them. And half the time this prevents the proper fertilization of the eggs you are desirous to hatch from this chosen stock.

One male with eight or ten hens will furnish you more certainly and regularly with impregnated eggs than you can obtain from a larger number, as a rule. Yet, if you desire to breed from two cocks to such hens, the two males should be of the same variety, and of equally good quality; and each may be placed with the hens upon alternate days, or weeks, during the season, to advantage. That is to say, with sixteen or twenty hens and pullets, kept by themselves, half in separate pens, the two cocks may be exchanged from week to week, from one pen to the other. We have found this a good and easily-managed plan.

With self-colored birds, such as pure white, buff, or black fowls, the points to consider in *mating* are those of fine carriage, perfect combs, symmetrical shape, fair size, moderate length of leg, broad, full breast, prime condition, and the absence of all foul feathers, discoloration of hackles, or any kind of deformity.

A "hump-backed" bird, or one carrying a "wry tail," showing foul feathers, a hatchet-shaped breast, with over long legs, deformed comb or beak, a "hollow back," or weak hock-joints, should never be used to breed from. These infirmities, visible to the eye always, are transmissable to the progeny ; and from such fowls good uniform chicks can never be reproduced.

With parti-colored birds, such as the Brahmas, the Spangled
Hamburgs, the Plymouth Rocks, the colored Games and
Bantams, etc., this matter of mating, for the reproduction
of prime specimens of their individual class, is a much
nicer and more difficult operation to manage, either successfully or satisfactorily.

It is only through repeated experiment, careful selection
of the best pointed and finest specimens in the first instance,
and good taste as well as some knowledge of what is to be
attempted subsequently, that the most desirable results can
be attained. And there are few secrets in fowl-breeding so
intricate, or so little understood generally, as is this process
of mating parti-colored stock judiciously, more particularly
in the work of breeding to color and feather.

Out of the hundreds of good breeders at this time in
America, some of whom raise large numbers of fine birds
annually, there are few men who either comprehend or practice this thing, nicely. They procure what is deemed first-
class stock, put their often dearly-bought birds together, and
are more or less fortunate in rearing promising chickens from
the connection, as they receive them from the seller.

But the fowls are frequently originally ill-mated in color
or points. And shortly the buyer finds that he has got more
than he bargained for in the progeny he produces from those
costly "imported" or "premium" samples, of one variety
or another, which do not breed accurately their cast of
plumage, etc.

No one who fancies fine stock can have a single year's
experience without noting how difficult it is to accomplish
his desired object in this respect, even with "the best" to
begin with. And few careful novices in the work of poul-
try-rearing are there, who do not quickly discover the value
of extreme caution and critical judgment in their efforts in
this *mating* of birds, to produce given results.

It is *all*-important, therefore, that shades of color in feathering, nice points in form and size, defined characteristics of

superior quality, developed evidences of fertility in the hens, and of stamina, robustness and vigor in the males, should be combined towards the promotion of accurate breeding. And these different qualities should all be brought to operate harmoniously with the two sexes, as well also as those of each upon the other, so that the highest degree of perfection in plumage, form, carriage, soundness and beauty, as well as usefulness, may be attained in a majority of the progeny produced from the contemplated union.

To effect this, and to carry out successfully such a mode of management, requires study, a love of the interesting work, and watchful care, as well as good taste and judgment.

By continuous experiment, through repeated trials, and from practical observation only, can the highest points be reached. To realize which, we propose to offer our views in these pages as to the best means that may be adopted for the consummation of this desirable object, which we have acquired some knowledge of through long and varied experience.

And to accomplish this result, we must again insist upon one point that is too often overlooked, or not properly appreciated. And this is the nice selection of the *sire* from which we attempt to breed.

It is quite beyond question the fact that the male bird is of the greatest consequence in this operation; for, through him is transmitted a majority of the more desirable qualities, if he be a good one.

He should not be over-sized, however — among the Cochins, and Brahmas, or the heavy colored Dorkings. A 14 or 15 pound cock is never a good breeder. He answers for the show pen, but is not the thing in your breeding runs. And however much the novice may admire these stalwart specimens, to look at, he should never undertake to breed such a bird, with the expectation of reproducing his like with averaged-sized hens or pullets.

A very nice thing to do, is the mating of parti-colored

fowls to produce a given cast of plumage in the progeny bred that shall be both what we aim to establish in a strain for color, and at the same time render the product thus obtained uniformly alike, or nearly so.

Sir John Seabright (or, more likely, his poultry-keeper) effected a very rare thing in his final accomplishment of the beautiful Golden and Silver-Laced Bantams he originated, and which will always bear his name, because there was never anything like them before; and nothing surpassing them in good blood, in general characteristics, in beauty and precision, has ever since been created.

The term "blood" or "blooded" animal, or fowl, has no meaning as applicable particularly to the natural crimson fluid that courses through the veins of the body. When we speak of a "blooded horse" for instance, we allude to the fact that his pedigree is good, and his origin may be traced back to an Arab sire, or Barb, for example.

A pure "blooded" bull, or ram, is simply one of a clearly distinct variety, or "strain"—inheriting from prime original stock, fixed and peculiar characteristics in style, form and stamina, which they can and do transmit to their progeny, in a similar marked degree. Thus with poultry. They are pure "blooded," when coming from a known established sire, or variety and breed closely like the originals; as the Games, the Brahmas, the Cochins, the Seabrights, etc.

But the "Seabright Bantams" were the result of long-tried and repeated experiments, in the hands of a skillful expert, who commenced his work with original wild or native East India stock, unquestionably; and who established the colors and markings of his exquisitely plumed Bantams almost "to a feather," finally—after many trials and several years' breeding, back and forth.

This beautiful result could not be attained in one year, or two, or five—or in ten seasons, thus perfectly. But it was effected, at last. And now we have this breed, as fine as the originals, all over England and America—the prettiest and most distinctive of all the pigmy races of domestic fowls in the known world.

Sir John's success in this direction was suggestive. Scores of fanciers on both sides of the Atlantic have first and last made similar attempts at fixing a distinct color of feathering and markings upon some of the larger varieties of domestic fowls — with a view (if successful) to establishing and naming a breed that might possibly prove popular, and saleable, as a distinct new variety.

To a certain extent this laudable aim has in one or two notable instances in later years succeeded, though the object is not yet quite perfected. And it will require still some years of very careful and studied mating and selecting, to *establish* the varieties now alluded to, *en permanence*.

For example, how many of the pure steel-gray Brahmas, strictly black and white in color and pencilling, which were originated in the yards of the author of this treatise, at Melrose, Mass., in 1852, and which were first exhibited at Birmingham, Eng., in 1853 and there named by Mr. Tegetmeier as "the new variety of *Dark* Brahmas," can be found in the United States or in England, among the thousands existing of this popular variety, to-day?

Yet *this* was a fixed variety. And in our hands — bred as we originally bred it — clean and uncontaminated with any other stock, for years after 1852 and '53, the clear bright even pure steel-gray pullets and mottled-breasted cocks came as regularly marked and as uniform in color as were those which "astonished and delighted English fanciers," when Mr. Burnham sent over to London his first samples of this beautiful breed; which no one ever claimed to have seen before, and which no one since has been able to produce from any stock that has succeeded these first ones, either in Great Britain or upon this side of the water.

The Plymouth Rocks are another instance of breeding to feather, through crossing of original strong-blooded fowls, and by subsequent careful selection and mating, to produce clear color and markings of plumage. Much has already resulted with these, in the right direction, so far. But they are yet imperfect, and the cast of plumage and color of legs desired are not yet fixed, by any means; although the Standard recognises them as a distinct breed. Undoubtedly, in time, these birds will produce their like, very accurately.

The accepted "American Standard of excellence" in poultry, of to-day, very clearly defines what is nearest to perfection in color and points, in every admitted distinct variety of domestic fowl. And although this high standard in breeding has not yet been *fully* reached, among the specimens which from time to time have been produced and adjudged from the yards of competitors at our exhibitions, we have in many instances approached very near this point of perfection, in later years.

Improvements may still be made, however. And the course to be followed towards complete success, eventually, will be herein explained, in our present details touching some of the prominent "secrets in poultry breeding."

ABOUT THOROUGHBRED FOWLS.

I shall not enter upon a critical analyzation of the probable results that follow the "crossing" of two or more distinct breeds of fowls, or attempt to decide what proportion of either blood thus crossed enters into the composition of the progeny bred from them.

I do not believe it possible for any man to state with any degree of exactness how much of the *Cochin*, for instance, may be embodied in a cross with a *Leghorn*, or a barn-yard fowl, after the chicken produced is grown. It may be half-and-half. It may be a quarter and three-quarters — or otherwise. The chickens through such crosses "take after" the hens, mostly, or the progeny may be most like the cocks used. There is no rule that will apply invariably, in this process;

though I do not forget that one or two modern writers on poultry affirm with great precision how many eighths, sixteenths, or thirty-second parts of the blood of *each* parentage enter into the composition of the chicks produced by such a cross. This is a little too fine for *me!* I have not been able, thus far in my experience to fathom this conundrum — and so I gave it up, years ago.

I do not deem this point of much consequence, any way. But we call such chickens "half-breeds," usually. Yet it frequently happens that a vigorous Cochin or Light Brahma cock, introduced into the common farm-yard, will so stamp his image upon the chicks that result from this introduction of fresh blood, that the first cocks raised from this union will show all the characteristics of the foreign male bird so fully developed as to make them appear *genuine* Cochins or Brahmas, to the inexperienced eye. But breed these chickens together, and *their* progeny will "throw back" to the original barn-yard parentage directly, and inevitably.

I am now writing of what is denominated *pure* breeding, and not about crossing fowls. This last process is very well, in its place. If the farmer or poulterer who raises stock for eggs and market-supply only, desires to improve his common dunghill flocks, he can do this with certainty by introducing to his hens "blooded" cocks of the Dorking, Brahma, Cochin, Dominique, or Leghorn varieties, etc.

But the fancier or amateur who desires to breed for competition at the public shows, for sales of modern improved breeding-stock, or to gratify his own pride and ambition to have good blood about him, must permit *no* amalgamation of varieties upon his premises.* I speak advisedly on this subject. The week he attempts this folly, the flocks he thus tampers with are contaminated, and can no longer be talked of as *pure* breeds.

* Mr. Felch criticises this opinion of mine, in a little work he recently printed. But all the standard authorities extant, to-day, agree with me on this point; and hundreds of experiments have proved my position the correct one. G. P. B.

It is possible that hens thus crossed, upon being again bred steadily to a cock of their own color and variety, may throw good chickens, mostly. But they can never be positively depended on, for purity, after such contamination. And this point we have incontestibly proven, by many an experiment — to our cost, in past years.

We always advise novices in poultry-breeding to begin with one pure variety, only. Cultivate this thoroughly, before trying another or more breeds. And this mode will invariably prove the most instructive and most satisfactory.

When we commenced breeding five and thirty years ago, we did as many have done since. We had at the start half a dozen kinds of fowls upon our premises. Within two or three years we had a dozen varieties — such as they were. Then came the "Cochin Chinas," the "Shanghaes," the "Brahmapootras" so called, the "Plymouth Rocks," (which we exhibited in Boston in 1849,) and then the "Cochins" (or Shanghaes) of all colors. These were bred by themselves, or together, for some years as everybody in those days bred fowls. And a "motley crew" we had around us as early as in 1848.

But when the "Gray Shanghaes" — thoroughbred from the start — came into our hands, from which superb native Chinese stock have descended the noble Light and Dark "Brahmas" of later days, we began to cultivate them in their purity, and subsequently bred them thus for many years, to profit and great satisfaction.

Thus, our long experience with one pure variety has taught us how important it is — if we would raise *good* birds in their purity of blood, and continue to do so — that we should adhere to the course prescribed by natural laws. The day we move aside from this wise rule of conduct in breeding any kind of live stock, we go astray, and irrevocably.

Especially will this disastrous result occur in fowl-breeding — as the principle involved is identical; and it is beyond question that any description of "thoroughbred," to be kept up to its original quality and purity, must be bred only by itself, or with its own species, clean. With *fowls*, when we attempt to cultivate any particular variety, we should therefore as has already been advised, first possess ourselves of what is nearest to a pure or clean-bred strain, of the kind we fancy for reproduction.

It will readily suggest itself to the most casual observer, on reflection, for instance, that if he desires to breed fine White Cochins, it would be altogether absurd to attempt to do this through the union of a White cock with Buff or Partridge colored hens. He must operate with pure *white* fowls, of both sexes; and he should ascertain also if possible, at the outset, that the stock he purchases is not — and never has been — intermingled with those of any other color.

Now this announcement is not so simple, or so trivial, as at first blush it may seem; for many tyros and amateurs do this very foolish thing, at the commencement, even now-a-days. And they often expect, from a good white crower mated with colored pullets, to obtain white chickens, as fine as may be the sire they chance to buy at random!

A vigorous thoroughbred cock will impress his chief characteristics upon the progeny of hens of almost any color, in the first brood produced from such connection. But the chickens are mongrels, nevertheless. I have seen very fairly pointed and good colored Light Brahma chickens produced from a prime full-bred Light Brahma rooster, mated to a flock of common variously-colored barn-yard hens. In the second year afterwards, the chickens coming from eggs laid by the pullets of this cross were like Jacob's coat — of many colors; and no two of either sex were at all alike. There was nothing thorough-bred in this process, or product, of course— and, in the nature of things, there could not be.

In these days of enterprise and enlightenment, the amateur in fowl raising who buys and breeds common stock of an indifferent or mixed character, will *from this* produce no birds that will afford him the slightest satisfaction, as he becomes better informed about the details of the object he has undertaken.

The poultry-cultivator of our time should have a clearly defined aim in view, at the beginning; and if he acquire some knowledge of the true principles of breeding fowls, before he embarks too largely to invest, or strike out for results, he will be the gainer in the end; and he may save time, money and patience, by going forward with his work understandingly — as far as may be.

Robert Bakewell of England, the originator of his famous breed of sheep, made a very handsome fortune by establishing a standard of his own in thorough-breeding — through careful selection and well-conceived mating of his stock — which he very cautiously weeded season after season, until he fixed his "strain" beyond farther present improvement. And we have in America to-day more than one ambitious fowl-cultivator, who has by a similar process of determined and discriminating judgment in selecting and mating from year to year, brought his strain of poultry to the point where it is rightfully esteemed "thorough-bred." But they have accomplished this only after years of experiment, and by closely following Nature's established and immutable law of production and pro-creation.

This law never halts, it never varies. The progeny always resemble the parentage — more or less. And with full-bred animals of both sexes, the young product can always be identified at a glance, by the initiated. There are, of course, many more secrets yet unknown regarding the workings of this law, than all that have thus far been made known. But sufficient is determined to warrant the assertion that there is but one way to produce "thoroughbreds" of any description of men, animals, or fowls; and this mode is to begin with, and continue to cultivate, *only* thoroughbred stock.

To produce thoroughbred fowls, then, the leading secret of the formula is to procure and cultivate only the *best* of the variety we choose to favor; and never to mix or amalgamate

these with any other variety, while we wish to have the product coming from them "pure" — bearing constantly in mind
this patent fact; that when a fowl (or animal) of any fixed
breed has once been pregnant to another of a different variety
and color, that fowl or animal is forever afterwards crossed;
and the original purity of its blood is lost, in consequence of
the connection with this other breed, or variety — as we shall
more fully explain, in our subsequent pages.

CLOSE BREEDING, FOR "POINTS,"

OR, what is termed among fanciers " nice breeding to points
and feather," is a secret, and somewhat of an art, in the
chicken-raising business.

After appropriate " mating " and proper " selection " of the
individual stock we determine to place together for the time
being, it becomes necessary to the successful production of
the progeny we desire shall result from this chosen union,
that great care be exercised towards confining these particular fowls entirely within their own quarters; and that no
other birds shall have access to their limits during the breeding season.

This course is absolutely essential to keep the stock free
from contamination through accidental " crossing " by birds
of our own, in other runs, or from connection with the cocks
of a neighbor. A single deviation from this method may
spoil a whole season's work for the fancier — in a day.

There are numerous theories advanced, we are well aware,
upon this mooted point. Good breeders (in a general way)
have held that hens are *not* injured by intercourse with
males of another variety, if a certain stated period of time be
allowed the hen to lay out the eggs which may have been
fertilized by one, before she consorts with a different male.

But, although we have no positively demonstrated information as to just how many eggs may be impregnated within
a given period — say in a week or a month, by any one cock

—yet the experience of the writer has convinced him that the eggs so fertilized are limited to a very small number, at any one time; not more than three or four.

Now to arrive at this decision clearly, involves the expenditure of much care and time, close observation, and repeated instances of experiment. It can only be accomplished by selecting pullets and hens of different ages, alive, while they are laying vigorously. These fowls must be slaughtered in their prime; and a critical examination of the condition of the egg, and maturing yolks in the oviduct of each bird, will at once decide how many, or how few, seemingly have been fertilized; as the small white germ of the future chicken (that would have been) is distinctly discernible in the top of each and every yolk that is *apparently* impregnated.

Beyond this demonstration, to what extent the "life-principle" of the male *may* be, or may have been secretly absorbed by the female, so as to cause future fecundation in other or more immature yolks, (which do not at this time exhibit the unmistakable evidence of fertilization), is a "secret" in fowl-reproduction which no one has fathomed, so far as *I* am informed.

In oft-repeated instances, however, I have taken hens from their nests, when in the act of laying — young and old — and have killed and dissected them immediately, to gather information upon this curious and interesting point.

The editor of the Poultry World in his magazine for 1876, upon this topic writes that "a domestic fowl's egg is a curious thing. If we examine this conformation critically, to learn in detail about its origin, its growth, its mature formation and what results from it subsequently, when set upon and hatched, no topic in nature is more interesting; no product of animal life is more marvelous to the student of nature, from its inception to the moment of the birth of the bird it produces. This secret process of incubation is very interesting, and few have more than a superficial idea of this operation, which we will briefly explain.

" At the close of the third day after the hen is set upon the freshly impregnated eggs, the lineaments of the chick's body faintly appear. The heart begins to beat the fourth day. At the end of the fifth day the wings and brain-globules show. The liver is seen on the sixth day, when the bill appears also. On the tenth day the feathers begin to show, and on the eleventh the eyes appear. On the fourteenth the stomach and lungs are perfected. On the fifteenth or six-teenth day the bill opens, often. At the eighteenth day it ' peeps,' and, growing rapidly stronger, breaks from its shell on the twenty-first day."

How astonishing, exclaims a noted English writer, that all the parts of an animal's body should be concealed within this egg, and require nothing but heat to unfold and quicken them into life — that the whole formation of the chick should be so constant and regular that exactly at the same hour all these changes will occur in the generality of eggs, and that the moment it is hatched, it is heavier than the egg was before!

Marvelous combination, indeed! Instructive lessons may be gathered from this simple operation, by him who watches the process of these manifold but always uniform changes and results. Yet there are numerous other wonders " hidden from our knowledge in this connection, of which, from our limited faculties, we must remain in ignorance."

There are indeed many intricacies, or secretly-wrought operations in the formation of the egg, which result in giving us the curious combination which contains the vital principle of an animated being. Yet very little is known, through actual, thorough experiment, of the details of the workings of this natural construction : so wonderful in its origin as well as through all its changes, from the infinitesimal vesicle form-ing at first in the ovary, down to the ejection of the perfect hard-shelled egg laid by the healthy hen, as may be seen through examining the following facts:

The ovary (or egg-sac) in the fowl, lies just in front of the left kidney. The passage from it, outward, is called the oviduct. The ovary contains the little globular germs of the eggs that are naturally formed with the early growth of the birds; and are very numerous, six or seven hundred (of various diminutive sizes) having been counted in young hens, less than a year old. And this gave rise to the theory that *all* the eggs a domestic fowl would ever lay in her life are formed at one time, in the first instance, in this embryo state.

These globules slowly increase in proportions, those lying nearest to the mouth of the oviduct enlarging first and passing out one by one into the passage, as they approach maturity. When the first or outer vesicle has become near the natural size of the common yolk, it is caught in the funnel-shaped end of the egg-passage; and each yolk, as it goes slowly down through this flexible tube, has formed about it the albumen or " white " of the egg. This substance contains fine strong threads in its composition, which hold the yolk in its place in the future shell. The membrane that lines the shell is then formed, and finally the outer hard shell. The " white " of the egg is first formed near the mouth of the oviduct; the membranes, half way down; the hard shell, last, at the lower end of this egg-passage.

Kill a vigorous laying-fowl any day when a year old, and carefully examine the ovary and oviduct. You will find *one* perfectly-formed hard-shelled egg ready to be laid, frequently; then a full-sized " soft-shelled " egg above it; then a smaller, membraneous-covered yolk above that; then a yolk two-thirds size, then half-size, then quarter-size, and, so on (from the upper portion of the egg-tube into and through the oviduct), still smaller embryo eggs or yolks; from the dimensions of a pea to those of finest mustard-seeds, or less, in bulk. Count all you can see, if you are curious, then apply the microscope and you may find five, six, seven hundred of these tiny vesicles, of various sizes, each of which would have formed a perfect hard-shelled egg in time.

These eggs are impregnated in the yolk after they enter the egg-passage, undoubtedly, and before the outer membraneous secretion (or white) is formed. How *many* are impregnated or rendered fertile at one time, is a question not yet decided. But the best authorities give as the most reasonable answer to this inquiry, that but very few are impregnated at the same moment; and that by the continuous association of the cocks with the hens, only, can the eggs laid be rendered available for successful hatching.

A few months after the above article appeared — as the result of half a dozen recent careful experiments in this direction — I communicated to the " Poultry World " papers which cover much of the settled confirmation of my opinion upon the question of original EGG-FORMATION and its *impregnation*, which I am confident has been hitherto a "secret" to most poultry breeders in America, since I have never met in print with any account like this; which so well-posted a writer on poultry as is H. H. Stoddard, of Hartford, recommended very kindly to the careful perusal of his numerous readers, as a "point of great interest to breeders and fanciers." This communication, with its accompanying illustration, I transfer to these pages by permission of Mr. S., in the next chapter.

EGG-FORMATION, IMPREGNATION, ETC.

THE secrets involved in the processes indicated by the title to this chapter, are perhaps known less of, by breeders generally, than are any and all other minutiæ connected with domestic fowl culture. The following was addressed by the author of this book to H. H. Stoddard, Hartford :

" SIR : — I was interested in a late editorial in your magazine upon the subject of the eggs of domestic fowls, their origin, formation, etc.

I have frequently experimented upon slaughtered hens and pullets of various kinds, and of different ages, with a view to ascertain, as nearly as possible, some of the intricacies or "secrets" you alluded to, in the breeding of poultry. This study has been to me of the greatest interest — though, as you suggested-our naturally limited faculties compel us to remain in ignorance of much of the wonderful economy of nature, combined in the simple object to which this communication refers. After reading your comments, I repeated recently what I have done many times before, with the following results:

I took from a flock of Partridge Cochins and Brown Leghorns, two hens —one two years and the other thirteen months old—upon which I experimented in this wise. (The fowls were both laying nicely, and the Cochin I took from the nest, in the act of laying.)

Having had them killed and dressed, I opened both carefully, cutting from the centre of the breast-bone backward to the top of the vent.

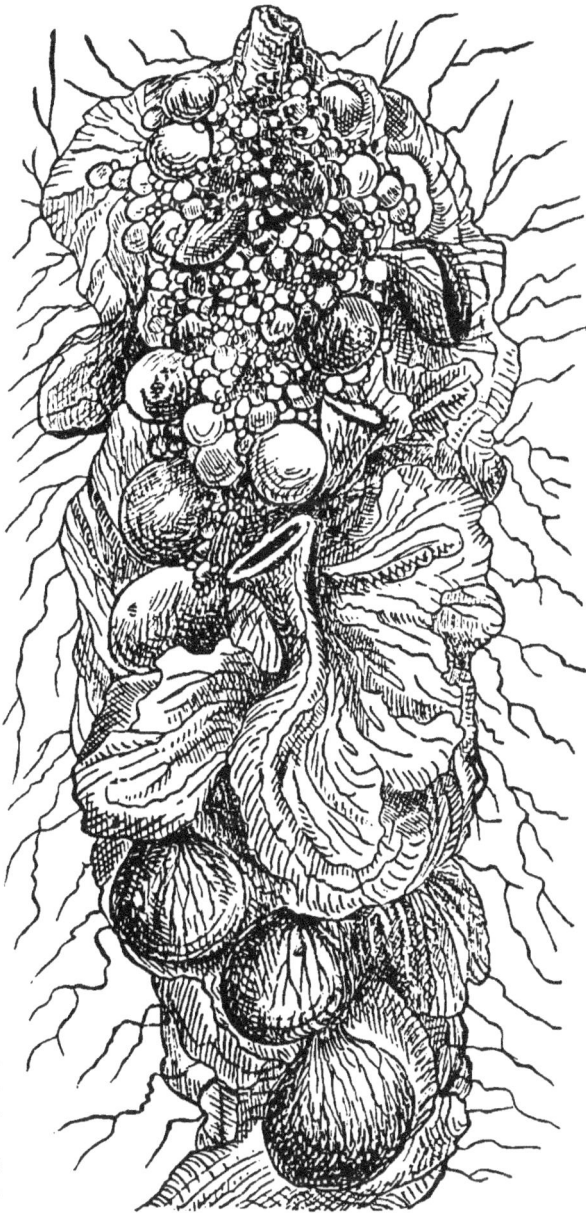

CONTENTS OF EGG-SAC.

Showing ova and partially developed yolks; with OVIDUCT detached, containing three impregnated yolks, in open lower tube. Taken from a laying Partridge Cochin pullet, eleven months old.

I found them rather fat (the two-year old Cochin particularly), but both were "full of eggs" of all sizes; from one just ready to be discharged, hard-shelled, to the minutest speck of a globule of pale yellow yolk.

In the lower end of the oviduct or egg-passage, outward, the mature shelled egg was formed, which the old hen was about to deposit in the nest when I removed her. Above this, towards the sac — in the egg-tube — I found four other eggs (yolks) ranging from full size gradually down to that of one the size of a boy's marble; and just at the open neck of the passage into the sac there was a fifth, the size of a filbert. The shelled egg I broke, and found it impregnated. The first and second were completely formed (or nearly so); yolks were also plainly fertilized. Beyond this I could discover nothing farther in this direction. I then took away and examined the sac itself.

If this egg-bag or ovary be in a healthy condition, and the fowl is laying vigorously, the ova can be counted clearly, at the cost of a little patience. This sac covers the embryo eggs. They are to be seen of all sizes *there* also, as well as in the oviduct, *en masse*. In the egg-passage there are never commonly more than three or four at a time, slowly passing out, as they mature most rapidly. As you state, the *white* forms in the centre of the passage, around each yolk separately, and the hard shell over all at the lower end of the tube, immediately prior to ejection, or laying.

Now, this hen had laid almost daily for several weeks. She was of a prolific race (and so was the Leghorn pullet). And thus we perceive how very rapidly the hard shell, and the albumen *previously*, must form in the egg-passage around the mature yolk, since one egg only was ready for depositing; and had she not been killed, the next fully-ripe yolk must have been "whited" and "shelled" within four-and-twenty hours afterwards, to have been laid as she usually laid her eggs, say five in a week, for several weeks previously.

In this egg-sac I found one hundred and eighteen perfectly formed yolks, the size of large peas, and down to that of turnip seed. Of the largest, there were seven or eight; of the medium size, as big as buck-shot, there were over twenty; of the rest, half this size; and then down to those as small as a pin's head and less. These were plain to the naked eye, connected together like bunches of grapes, mostly, which masses I separated and counted, one by one. Then I took up the three or four vesicles attached to the three upper ends of this egg-mass, which little pouches (or minor bags) secured each to the mass, are flattened, fig-shaped, and are about as large as a lady's finger-nail. These are filled with ova again; but the globules they contain are infinitesimal in size. (See engraving, page 21.)

I examined these tiny sacks, or vesicles, by opening and carefully scraping out the contents with a thin pocket-knife blade, and this matter I placed under my microscope. Each small sack contained about the same quantity of substance, and all appeared like the finest smelt or trout-spawn at first, but under the glass the whole became defined. The contents proved minute *yolks* again. I separated these with the point of a fine cambric needle (while under the lens,) and then counted them — though imperfectly, they were so very delicate; but in each little sack there were nearly one hundred (eighty to ninety) of these separate particles, or embryo yolks.

The hen thus experimented with had laid in 1875, about one hundred and sixty or one hundred and seventy eggs. She began late in December last to lay again, and up to May she had laid over a hundred eggs more. The mature and immature yolks found in her, numbered over one hundred and thirty, including those in the egg-sac; while those in the four minor sacks, microscopically determined, would, by count, reach, at the least, three hundred and seventy-five to four hundred miniature yolk globules.

She had laid, in less than two years, towards three hundred eggs. She had t' e yolks formed and forming clearly within her (when slaughtered) ,i five hundred and thirty more, large and small. If these were 'all the eggs which nature would furnish for her natural life, there would have been, in all, eight hundred to nine hundred eggs, which this Cochin hen would have laid, first and last, say in four or five years from hatching, had she lived so long.

This conclusion is based upon the old theory that all the eggs a hen will *ever* lay in her life, are formed (in embryo) at one and the same time, in the first place; and that when this " foreordained " quantity is all matured and ejected, by natural process, the hen will cease to lay, altogether. This may require three, four, or six years to accomplish. But when the ovary is exhausted of the primal original deposit of egg-germs natural to its capacity, the hen stops laying; and though she may grow to be as old as Joyce Heth, no more (or no new) ova will ever be generated in *her* " egg-sack."

In the instance of the Brown Leghorn, dissected the same day, the result was very similar, and will not require to be detailed — except to note her *age*, and the fact that there were a larger number of embryo eggs found in this subject. This hen had been laying since January, very generously. In the oviduct I found six formed yolks, from full size to that of an ounce bullet. In the egg-sack there were first massed about 200 globules of yolk, of all sizes; from that of a large pea down to that of mustard-seed. Attached to this main (partially developed) mass, as in the Cochin case, there were *seven* distinct small closed sacks or bags, one of which, examined under the glass, turned out nearly 150 diminutive particles of incipient ova, or minute yolks.

The other six (of the seven) small sacks were less in size than the first; but all were charged with this kind of spawn, still more imperfectly developed. But it was evident that there was the foundation for a greater *number* of eggs in the Leghorn, than in the Cochin, had she lived long enough to have allowed them to mature, and laid them all.

The formation of the *interior* arrangement of the oviduct or egg-sack was precisely alike in both birds, however — as it was like all others I have examined critically; that is, the connected *mass* of egg-bags inside the ovary-cover was independent of the sack-lining, and these minor bags were strung together; the largest or most developed mass, being near the mouth of the ovary, whence the eggs are first sucked out, one after another, into the egg-passage, towards maturing.

A third experiment, which I made at the same time, resulted similarly, thus: I selected one of my own Light Brahma pullets, eleven months old, for this purpose, on the day succeeding the previously-described cases. She was in fine condition, and weighed before killing, 9 lbs. 5 ozs. She had laid one litter of about thirty eggs, and had commenced upon her second laying, three weeks previous to being slaughtered.

I found in the lower end of the oviduct of this pullet, one hard-shelled egg, ready to be ejected; in the oviduct (or egg-tube) above this, there were three full-sized yolks, and two about two-thirds grown. At the mouth of the passage from the sack there were two more, nearly as large. Directly inside the egg-sac there were three others — these last five yolks being from half-size to that of a ripe Isabella grape. Thus, in all, there were nine full and half-grown yolks or eggs maturing — separately from the general mass or clusters *within* the ovary.

Next beyond these came a first cluster of ova in a mass, twelve of the size of small peas, and so on down to that of hemp-seed, or less; numbering seventy-two distinct yolks, without the twelve largest. Beyond this was a second bunch or mass (attached by fine ligaments to the others), of lesser size — say from that of a buck-shot, down — numbering one hundred and twenty-eight vesicles. A third mass, still smaller in average size, lay beyond this, in the sack, in which were visible one hundred and twelve of the yolk globules; and above these there were three minor bunches (or inner sacks) containing undeveloped ova; which latter, under the microscope, consisted clearly of the diminutive pale yellow yolks again, about one hundred to one hundred and ten in each sack.

Thus, in the Light Brahma pullet's case, her first litters numbered about one hundred and forty eggs, including those she had laid and those found in the oviduct and first cluster, after killing. This, by nearly accurate count, would give as the whole number of eggs this fowl would have laid (had she lived to discharge them naturally), about seven hundred and thirty to seven hundred and fifty in all; which, I think, is under rather than over, the ordinary average whole *number* of eggs to be found, in some stage of development, at one time, in the sac and oviduct of a full-grown hen, when ready to lay her first egg.

As in the first-mentioned experiment herein noted, this Brahma pullet had but three eggs, or yolks (the perfect hard-shelled one among them), which I could discover were fecundated. To what extent the vital principle of the male *may* have operated on other yolks present in this pullet, or how much of this subtle element injected by the cock may, from time to time, or at any time, be secretively absorbed through natural reproductive laws by the hen, I think it impossible to determine. And I am of the opinion that none of us ever have, or ever can, solve *this* "secret in fowl-breeding."

The full details of my fourth experiment (upon a thirteen-months old Cochin) need not be added here, except to say that, in all particulars, the result of my experiment was, in this case, identical with the other three, with this single exception; I found in the oviduct, two-thirds the way down from the egg-sack towards the vent, a full-grown impregnated yolk, with the white or albumen half formed around it.

This yolk contained the opaque white spot at the top, indicating fertilization, and around it had formed the albumen in a transparent state. Outside of this incasement of albumen, the whole was inclosed in a very thin membraneous sack as fine and sheer as a cobweb, but very strong in fibre. The fowl had laid an egg the day previous to killing, and this one was rapidly approaching perfection, evidently, and would have been laid on the day following had she not been slaughtered. There were five half-sized and smaller yolks in the oviduct, besides this more advanced one; and this with one other yolk next above it in the great tube, only was fertilized, that I could discover. The contents of the egg-sac and the sack itself were like all the rest — this pullet having, in imperfect ova and more developed yolks of all sizes, over seven hundred globules in her ovary; and she had been laying finely for months.

There is no doubt in my mind of three things to wit; Not more than three or four yolks or premature eggs are ever impregnated at a time, in advance. The white of the egg is formed around the yolk in the egg-passage, or oviduct, and the shell at its lower extremity, in twenty-four to thirty-six hours; and lastly, that all the eggs a domestic fowl will or can lay during her whole life, are started at once, in embryo, originally in the ovary, be this quantity more or less.

And finally, I am confirmed in my belief that, however these lesser sacks may mature (that is, whether each fully develops from year to year, or more than one in a year) no *new* minor sacks form after the first mass is established prior to the laying of the pullet at all. And no matter how long she may live, that after all these ova shall be formed into eggs and are ejected, she will lay no more.

The engraving given on page 21 is good. The upper sack — laid open, be it understood — discloses the ordinary contents of a hen's ovary when in laying condition and in full health. The lower portion, from the neck of the ovisac to the *cloaca*, is detached, and shows its funnel-shaped mouth at top. Below this runs the irregularly-formed tubular oviduct, in which the egg-yolks mature and drop slowly down this passage, as they enlarge and ripen before reaching the lowest point.

In this extreme lower duct, which is naturally dilated to hold the fully-formed shell as it enlarges, the latter is completed: and when ripe, the egg is excreted, in its hard white covering, from this *cloaca*, or final receiver, and dropped into the nest.

I have this year tested another experiment, thus: I reserved from my Light Brahma flock of 1875 pullets, *one* late fowl that had never been associated with a male bird at all. She began to lay at seven and one-half months old. When she had laid about a dozen eggs, each one of which I broke and found unfertilized, I killed and dissected her.

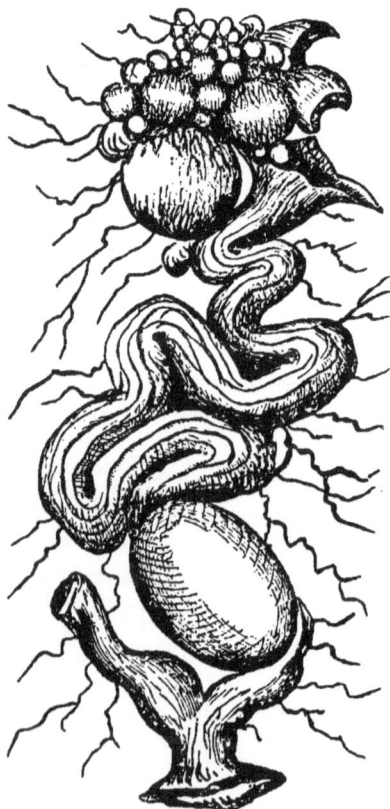

The *cloaca*, or final receiver of the egg, just before the latter is laid.

In her oviduct I found a mature egg ready to be discharged that day, and two other yolks nearly grown. Above (in the upper end of the egg-passage) I found two other yolks as large round as a small walnut. But not one of these four yolks showed the impregnated white spot to be seen in all the mature yolks found in the other slaughtered birds described. Of course I did not expect to discover this demonstration, since no cock had ever been permitted to associate with this hen.

But what I *did* ascertain, convincing to my mind, was, that the indication of fertility of a fowl's egg is apparent *only* when this white speck is to be seen at the outer edge of the yolk; a circumstance which has for years been declared by many writers to be uncertain, or of no consequence. I maintain that whenever this clearly perceptible opaque white spot is *absent*, the egg is worthless for setting. It is positively infertile. The fact of the presence of this substance in the yolk, or not, may be determined with the common "egg-tester," or by holding the egg to the eye, with a sharp light directly behind it, in a dark closet or room.

I deem the facts here stated on the formation and fertilization of fowl's eggs both instructive and conclusive, as well as interesting. Such are the results I have reached through considerable care, and from numerous actual experiments now described. And to arrive clearly at these results requires patience, close study, varied experiments, the sacrifice of many valuable birds just at the time when they are in their best trim and greatest usefulness, and some knowledge of fowls, their habits, their qualities, and their construction.

From these accurate statements it will be seen that in no instance among the half dozen hens chosen in the full vigor of fertility for experiment, did the oviduct contain more than four (and most of them only three) apparently fecundated eggs, or yolks, when the fowl was slaughtered. And we are constrained to believe, from these and many prior similar experiments and results, that only three or four of the extreme outer, or *lower* yolks in the oviduct, are impregnated at any one time, prior to the eggs being perfected and laid.

Yet notwithstanding all this, there come other indications of an important character in our experience, which point to the probability that although we cannot *see* the above mentioned evidence of fertilization with the naked eye, upon more than three or four yolks at a time, within the oviduct or outer egg-passage — the life-principle of the cock may, as we have suggested, penetrate or permeate the linings of both tube and sack, imperceptibly. Or, by natural absorption, the fluid may be taken up by the hen, and it may pass over and around the lesser yolks, or even into the egg-sack, where the first masses of diminutive vesicles are found, in such numbers, of all sizes. And here these latter mentioned undeveloped yolks and ova *may* be fertilized, for aught that is known with any degree of positiveness. Still, we know that a white hen, for example, bred to a white cock for the whole or part of a season, and then bred with a black male for a few weeks, will give us eggs that will hatch only speckled, patched, or black chickens, *very soon after the change of cocks is made.*

Now, if any considerable number of eggs are fertilized *at a time* (say with the first cock, in the outset, whose chickens from the white hen come regularly *white*, prior to the change of males) how does it occur that the spotted or black chickens make their appearance from this same hen's eggs, laid within a week after the exchange of cocks? Surely no sane man will maintain that this white hen's eggs are fecundated *twice* — or first by one cock, and then by the other!

Therefore we are again confirmed in our judgment that but very *few* yolks are fertilized at a time; and these only after they pass *out* of the egg-sack into the oviduct, half or two-thirds grown in bulk, and *prior* to the gathering of the albumen around each yolk, which is found in or near the centre of the lower tube, on its way downward to the vent.

But all this is an unsolved problem. And so we are compelled to accept what follows the connection of the selected male and females, and improve upon this product subsequently as best we can — while we may set *this* down as true; that if we remove the male bird altogether from the hens, *after* the third or fourth yolk is thus fertilized, (and keep him away from them,) eggs laid subsequently to that third or fourth one will not usually produce chickens during the cock's absence, if set under the hen. This we have tried, over and over again —with almost unvarying results.

Now, when the cock is returned to his hens, the first two or three eggs that are immediately thereafter laid will also be barren, and worthless for purposes of incubation. This fact we have determined, from numerous experiments, which have aided to show us that it is the nearly perfect *yolk* that receives the impregnation; and that this occurs *before* the " white " or albumen forms around it, in the centre of the oviduct.

During the absence of the cock from his mates, the yolks continue to mature as usual, one after another; but, being unfertilized, they must be discharged from the oviduct in this condition; since it is simply impossible to fecundate the hard-shelled egg, of course, (when ready to be laid) or the yolk above this in the oviduct, around which the solid " white " is formed, with its transparent but tough outer envelope; which encases the albumen and subsequently unites with the inner membrane of the hard shell.

To be precise, let us observe here that if we return the same cock, or as perfect a specimen as he is, of the same variety and color, to the hens he was taken from, there will be no noticeable change in the progeny that comes from this reunion, probably. But if we meanwhile introduce in place of the original a cock of a different color or breed, the eggs laid by the hens within a week afterwards will produce, in hatching, a " cross " or mongrel, inevitably.

If you then remove *this* male, and restore your original pure-bred bird to the same hens, within another week the eggs those hens lay will give you chickens more or less outwardly like the parentage — at first : but the hens that have associated for however few days with the second cock, will be thus forever " crossed." And no subsequent hatchings of their eggs can *ever* again be depended on to give you the pure blood and plumage of the original cock and hens.

This reasoning in some measure seems to be paradoxical, I know. For, if the changed cock impregnates but a few of the eggs, as we assume, how is it that the white hen's chickens long afterwards should come black or spotted — when replaced in union with her original white mate ?

This is what I am unable to explain, and this curious secret has never yet been explained, in poultry or animal breeding. Yet the *fact*, as herein set down, remains. This continual cropping out of spotted chicks from a white hen's eggs *once* bred to a colored cock, during her entire subsequent existence, follows as surely and as inevitably as that she continues to lay eggs in her future. And the contamination is never eradicated.

Why this so follows the crossing mentioned, we may never know. But in scores of instances, from watchful personal experiment, we have found this result invariable, and certain.

It may perhaps be appropriately stated here, that the most successful result in *uniformity* of production is realized in breeding from one strain or line of ancestry, direct. A prime vigorous cock being selected, (one possessing all or a majority of the fine qualities we seek to perpetuate), and this male being bred to a few hens of the same type and the best of their kind, will give us in the first progeny very uniformly good chickens.

The pullets among this product, if bred back to the old cock, will also give us a majority of good chickens. The *hens* only, for a couple of years, should be bred to the original cock, or a cock in the third remove from him. The *cocks* of the first result cannot be used advantageously with any of these hens or pullets — for nicest breeding.

If more hens are wanted, fresh female blood should be now introduced; and one or two of the best cocks from this last union may be bred back with the second hens (at two years old) to advantage. This plan avoids close in-and-in breeding, which is detrimental, always.

Select from all of your flocks only the best birds, at any time. Mate them carefully, for *color*, and avoid as much as possible (however promising individual birds may be) the breeding together of cocks and pullets of the same age, or those which come from eggs laid by the same hen. Brothers and sisters make but indifferent breeders; and their chicks rarely prove valuable for after mating, at the best.

But, for the reasons given, we repeat that *for close clean breeding* we must keep our chosen cock and hens strictly by themselves, and to themselves. The females should never be permitted to receive the attentions of a strange cock, in any instance. And thus alone can they remain "pure" breeders, provided always that they are uncontaminated in the first place, when mated, as we have directed.

The real secret of all the blemishes, "sports," discolored plumage, and imperfectly feathered chickens produced from what are so often purchased for "pure bloods," is traceable to the error we have now explained — at some time in their lives with themselves or their progenitors — committed by previous owners, through wrong management.

This result follows a law of nature that is immutable, and universal, in the work of procreation ; and however the point may be argued as to its wherefore, *all* experience points to this result, whenever the experiment now considered has been ventured upon, where different breeds are kept by the same poultry cultivator.

If we desire to keep only *one* flock of hens however, upon the premises, we may have a portion of them of non-setting varieties — say Leghorns or Black Spanish, for the production of eggs, and a portion of pure Brahmas or Cochins, to use as incubators. An easily managed plan.

Breed these with one vigorous pure cock, and set such of the eggs as you may choose. The *color* of the shells will indicate whence they come — since the Leghorns, &c., are white shelled, and the Asiatics are more or less tinted in color. This obviates the necessity of separating the varieties into different flocks (where you have but limited space for their accommodation), and a part of your eggs will thus be " pure-bred," for subsequent setting ; if the cock and half the hens are of the same sort.

In the matter of *crossing* fowls, herein explained, it is precisely thus with pigeons, with domesticated cage-birds, with cattle, horses, sheep, dogs, rabbits — *all* animal creation. It has been thus from time immemorial. It will always remain so — because the prime laws of Nature are unchangeable.

Therefore, if we aim to reproduce any given kind or style of fancy stock which we hope to see like its progenitors, we must not only procure the parentage as nearly in its purity as it may be possible to obtain, but — when we get such stock, be it poultry or otherwise — we must continue to breed it, uncontaminated, from first to last. And this "secret" is among the most important of all, in good close breeding.

That unsightly and annoying excrescence, the " falcon *hock*," which has been bred upon Light and Dark Brahmas in

England and sent over to the United States within the past seven years, well illustrates our point touching the contamination of poultry stock, by injudicious or careless experiments in breeding.

Upon the high-priced fancy birds of the above named varieties, and also on some strains of English-bred Buff and White, as well as Partridge Cochins, this execrable deformity made its appearance among the importations of Messrs. Herstine, Van Winkle, Philander Williams and others, a few years since.

They bred and disseminated this stock here until it came to be an eye-sore in hundreds of American yards. The new Standard first declared this hock "highly objectionable," and then pronounced it a "disqualification" for exhibition birds — and justly, too.

This "secret" has cost them many good dollars to learn, and more than one ambitious American fancier has now discovered that it was far easier to put this beastly hock upon the shanks of his otherwise good Asiatics, than it is to work it off again, when he desired! It can *never* be altogether eradicated, where it once exists. And for this reason, a falcon-hocked bird should never be used as a breeder.

A very desirable "secret" to acquire is a knowledge of the successful mode that may induce fowls to lay well. Indeed, if it were possible to adopt any system that might tend to effect so important a result, which would "make hens lay" more promptly, more generously, and more regularly than they do, or might, under ordinary good treatment — the discovery would be most acceptable to farmers and breeders everywhere, unquestionably.

We have tried many experiments with this object in view, and we have found that both yearling pullets and adult birds can be stimulated to an increase of egg-laying for a time, very readily. But this is accomplished at the cost of their health and their longevity.

Hens thus forced, unnaturally, will deposit more eggs *in a given time*, by thirty to fifty per cent. That is, when fed upon stimulating egg-producing food regularly and continually, they will lay in a single season a third more eggs than they will under ordinary care and feed; and these eggs will be deposited in a shorter period, annually, than if they are fed only in the common way. But this increased production destroys the birds in a year or two, or renders them sterile, after the second or third season.

Still, hens may be thus forced to advantage, *as layers* — since they may be killed off, after the second year, for marketing, when they give out as egg-producers; and the owner will have realized (through such extra feed) in the first two seasons of their lives, what he must have waited for three years, at least, in the usual course. In this way he will get from such birds the bulk of all the eggs Nature provides them with — and by slaughtering these, and renewing his laying stock, he will save a year or two of feeding to comparatively no profit.

You "cannot have your cake and eat it, too," in this matter, however. And if you force the hens to lay their four or five years' supply of eggs in two or three seasons — there comes the end. And you gain *in time*, simply, by this stimulating means.

English poulterers have for years followed this method, and various sorts of patented egg-producing stimulants are prepared and sold largely in Great Britain, as well as for exportation. These preparations have been found both economical and advantageous; and among our home manufactures for this purpose, the "*Imperial Egg Food*" now made in Hartford, Conn., by Cha's. R. Allen, has taken a high rank in the esteem of leading American poultrymen, who have used it extensively in the last year or two, and who uniformly certify to its wonderful properities in increasing the production of eggs among their flocks.

There is no doubt the use of this prepared food, properly given, will many times over repay its cost to farmer or poulterer, in the egg-product obtained. But we do not commend this (or any similar method) for use, where fowls are kept for fancy, or breeding purposes, strictly. Hens so forced will lay many eggs, but they are not the best for hatching purposes, we have found. And it is a settled point that no such excessive over-draught upon Nature as follows through this stimulating process, can be made without a corresponding drawback, in *some* way, in the health or lives of the hens thus fed.

There is one secret I have myself never yet been able to fathom, which in recent poultry magazines I see it claimed *could* be disclosed by some one out West, who affirms that he has " discovered" the key to. This is the mystery of the *sex* of fowls' eggs.

Although as we have stated, none can determine by seeing the shell, which sex of chicken may issue from it when the egg is hatched, yet it is quite possible, through certain methodical management in mating adult breeding-fowls, to obtain from their eggs a majority of one sex or the other, in the product.

A few years ago, a whole season's hatchings of Light Brahma chicks in our own yards — numbering nearly six hundred birds — yielded us three-fourths *cockerels*. And that same year, a score of our patrons to whom we sent eggs for incubation, reported like results. "All cocks, no pullets, scarcely," they declared.

Next season we changed the matings in our breeding-pens, entirely; and for a year or two had average good success, so far as the sex of our birds was concerned.

In 1874, we bred over four hundred chicks, in conjunction with Mr. Weymouth, and that year we raised less than forty cock-chickens, all told. About eighty-five per cent. proved pullets; some were fine, most of them fair, only.

Individually, we do not deem it of consequence to know (if we could) what are to be the sexes of the chicks we may produce — since Nature herself regulates this thing pretty evenly, ordinarily. But if in mating fowls for breeding, we put together birds of the two sexes that agree well; who incline to enjoy each others' society; and if we keep them quiet, peaceable, free from alarm by day or by night; if they are well fed, and cared for systematically — a large majority of *pullets* will be the result of such unions — each sex taking kindly to their nominal "affinity," during the breeding season.

If, on the other hand, we place strange birds together; or introduce imperious abusive cocks among the pullets; or cultivate noisy uneasy spunky hens, of the virago tribe, or have either sex that are vicious or towering in temper and habit — or quarrelsome and unhappy, during the periods of co-habitation — the issue from the eggs of such *mis*-mated and mis-matched fowls will be *cocks*, seven times in ten, out of a thousand hatched from stock thus injudiciously placed in compulsory union together. And this secret we have proved, over and over again, in our experience.

But it is unnecessary to enlarge upon this topic, here. No man can tell positively which contains one or the other sex, from any outward indications. All the numerous experiments tried with this or that shaped egg, with a view to discover its sex, upon any hypothesis whatever, have been and will be totally fruitless.

We have had the old theory that roundish smooth shells hold the pullets, and that the long or pointed ones will hatch cocks. This was found to be a fallacy. Then we had the air-bag theory, at one side or other of the shell-ends — which, inclining right or left, indicated one sex or the other, sure. This proved to be utterly valueless, as a guide to this secret.

Then a writer set forth the idea a few years since that weight (for size) was a positive thing; the *heaviest* fresh laid eggs containing cocks, and the *light* ones, (from the same hens or breed), holding the embryo pullets. This assumption turned out to be nonsense.

Then came the novel plan of an Englishman, who affirmed that if the eggs were dropped into a vessel of tepid or blood-warm water, soon after they were laid, a part would sink with the large ends turning downwards, These would hatch cocks. Those that turned small ends downward, held females germs — he declared. Thousands of eggs were set upon this recommendation, but no one ever succeeded in determining anything, through this stupid proposition.

Then the discovery was made by a Yankee that if you gathered your fresh laid eggs in a straw hat, (it must be a *straw* hat) and shook them up vigorously, those found at the top of the mass and set, would give male birds, while all underneath would be found to contain pullets.

Either one of these modes of discovery is quite as certain as the other ! And when we are able to determine from outward demonstrations prior to birth what is the sex of the mare's coming foal, the cows' approaching calf, the ewe's maturing lamb, or the unborn child in the woman's womb — we may be able possibly to *guess* what the sex of the chicken is, in the un-hatched egg.

This is one of the " secrets " (whatever quacks may promise to develope), which we opine will forever remain unrevealed to the most ardent experimentalist in our humble profession. And all we can ever know, as to whether an egg will produce a cock-chicken, or a pullet, we shall ascertain satisfactorily only when the bird bursts its little shell-prison, and reveals the fact *in propria persona.* For an egg is only an egg. And, whatever theorists or pretenders may assume regarding this " discovery," gentle reader — pray don't you forget this simple fact.

FACTS AGAINST SPECULATIONS.

In a foot-note to page 12 of the present edition of this work on the
"*Secrets in Fowl Breeding*," we briefly allude to a criticism which Mr.
I. K. Felch (in his lately published "*Amateur's Manual*") has thought
proper to make upon the principle we have for years been clearly satisfied was the true one, regarding the contamination of a female animal
or fowl, by an accidental or intentional temporary union with one of the
opposite sex that is *of a color or variety not its own.*

In response to that criticism, the author of this volume sent to the
"Poultry World," in October 1877, a paper which explains itself, and
which is inserted here, substantially, in support of my position set forth
in this work, to the effect that "the fancier who desires to breed fowls
for competition at our Public Shows, or for sales of modern improved
poultry breeding-stock—must permit NO *amalgamation of varieties upon
his premises.* For, the week he attempts this folly, the flocks he thus
tampers with are contaminated, and can no longer be talked about as of
pure blood."

Mr. Felch objected to this, in his book. And below I transfer to
these pages what I had to say in support of my doctrine; which so
pleased the great mass of breeders, that since its publication I have received scores of complimentary letters from all directions, approving
my theory *in toto*, and in many cases offering me the details of their
own personal experiments in support of my assertions — the result of
which, *with poultry*, have proven to their satisfaction, beyond a shadow
of doubt, that I am correct and that the opposite assumption is utterly
fallacious. The article mentioned was published under the title that
heads this chapter, and was as follows : —

H. H. STODDARD, *Sir :* — Mr. Felch, in a little book entitled the
"*Amateur's Manual*," which he has lately published, alludes to one of
my new volumes, thus : — "There is *no* chance, as the author of '*Secrets in Fowl Breeding*' asserts, for the dam (hen) to be contaminated
by a chance connection with a male not of her breed." And "there
can be *no* grounds for belief that a dam copulating with a sire of a different breed, has lost her purity of blood." And "we do not wonder
(if he believe this) that he asserts, in the commencement of his work,
that we have no absolutely thorough-bred fowls." And, he adds, "there
can be *no* contamination of the blood, or breeding of the dam, from this
cause," etc.

I was rather surprised at this doctrine from Mr. Felch. But, let us see. I cite below some twenty good authorities and scientists, whose many practical personal experiments in breeding are here truthfully recorded, who " believe " what I do, and what I have *proved*, beyond a possible doubt; that this " assertion " of mine in " *Secrets* " is the *only* true doctrine, and the *only* possible result that can follow a connection of a human being, an animal or a fowl, of one variety or species, copulating with that of another sort, color, or species. It is Nature's universal law. And this is constant, unchangeable, unalterable, immutable.

I doubt if he can point to a single case on record, where any female fowl or animal has been thus crossed " by chance " or in any other manner, with a breed and color *not its own*, that ever recovered its original purity, subsequently. In support of this (my) doctrine, I briefly refer Mr. Felch, and those who " believe " in his utterly untenable speculations, to the following facts and authorities, upon this subject.

Messrs. Corbie and Botard tried many experiments with pigeons, in this way — and they found that not in a single instance, after the first crosses of Carriers upon Nuns, and *vice versa* (male and female) could they obtain, from returning to the *original* stock, a single pure-colored or feathered bird from *either* of the once so-crossed varieties.

Mr. Darwin, in his " *Variations in Plants and Animals* " (a most exhaustive work on this point), lays down this principle: " The reproductive system is highly susceptible to changes in the conditions of life. But, among the rays of light which we may catch on this subject, this is an important one, namely: the clearly apparent influence of the male *first* having fruitful intercourse with the female, upon her *subsequent* offspring bred from *other* males."

This principle is clearly demonstrated every season in the year, among breeders of horses, cattle, sheep, swine, rabbits, dogs, etc., and it has been practically decided by Moubray, by Botard, by Bakewell, by Corbie, and by numerous other scientists, in experimenting with fowls, birds and pigeons.

Mr. James McGillivray, a noted Scotch veterinary surgeon, has stated very sensibly that " when *once* a pure animal of *any* breed has been pregnant to an animal of another breed, such pregnant animal " (and I say, *fowl*) " *is a cross forever; incapable* of ever producing pure progeny, afterward, from or of any breed."

Sir Edward Holmes relates this fact: " A young chestnut mare, seven-eighths Arabian blood, belonging to the Earl of Morton, was covered by a quagga (a kind of African wild ass), by way of experiment. The quagga was marked like a zebra, and the hybrid colt was similarly colored. The mare was thus served but once — in 1815. In 1817, 1818, and 1821, two, three and six years afterward, the same mare, from a full-bred black Arabian stallion, had three colts, and *all* bore the unequivocal bars and markings of the quagga, though the mare had not seen him since 1815.

Mr. Tegetmeier, noting the changes that occur frequently in croppings-out of strange-colored plumage upon what are esteemed "pure-bred fowls," refers to them as instances of reversion to a color or characteristic possessed by some ancient progenitor of the family —to which they "throw back." *I* contend, in such cases, that *the quagga has been round*, where these "pure" fowls have had their runs, at some previous time — we wot not when.

What is known, nowadays, as the pure Himalayan rabbit, is of a snow-white skin, with black ears, nose, tail and feet; and it produces its like, very accurately. Yet this race is known to have been made by a union of *silver-gray* rabbits. But, if the Himalayan doe be covered with a sandy or drab-colored buck, silver-gray rabbits are the product. An evident "reversion" to one of the *first* parents, again — as in the case of the strong-blooded quagga.

Six years ago, I published my "*New Poultry Book*," in which there is a chapter on this breeding-for-purity question. Mr. E. W. Barnes, of Plymton, read it, and three years ago he allowed a neighbor's Brown Leghorn cock to pass three days among his pen of eight one-year-old Light Brahma pullets, "for experiment's sake," he said. The Brown Leghorn cock was removed, and he has never once had anything on his premises since, but the Light Brahmas of both sexes — "pure." From the eggs set within a week after the Brown Leghorn cock was sent home, a third of the chicks when hatched, came brown, speckled-brown, or patched with brown, that same summer. Out of the eight hens, he saved four (which were alive a year ago), and last season — two years after the Brown Leghorn cock was dead — more than one-quarter of Mr. Barnes' chicks, bred from the old Light Brahma hens, with a Light Brahma cock *only*, since, came spotted, specked, and splashed with *brown* feathers. Mr. B. is satisfied that the quagga has been there! And so am *I*.

Mr. Goodale of Maine, author of "*Glimpses of Physiological Laws involved in the Reproduction of Animals*," etc., cites many cases in point, thus — in brief: "In several foals bred in the English Royal stud, got by the famous horse 'Acteon,' there appeared unmistakable marks of another stallion called 'Colonel,' of a different style and color. The dams of these colts, it was found, had all been bred to the 'Colonel' a year or two previously. . . . A colt got by 'Laurel' so resembled another horse named 'Camel,' that it was rumored that the foal must be 'Camel's.' It was ascertained that the dam had been served by 'Camel' the previous year. . . . Alexander Morrison had a fine Clydesdale mare served by a Spanish ass, and produced a mule, in 1843. She afterwards had a foal by a full-bred horse — but this second colt was very much like a mule, and, at a short distance, was taken for one. His ears were 9 1-2 inches long, and he stood over 16 hands high. He was a fine animal and highly prized. But his mother never got rid of the impress the Spanish ass made upon her progeny, then, or afterward. . . . An Aberdeen heifer in Forgue, was covered by a Teeswater bull, which

produced a fine cross-calf. Next year, this same cow was served by
one of her kind — a full-bred Aberdeenshire bull. The product was a
cross, again. At two years old it had long horns — while both the
'Aberdeen' parents were hornless animals. . . . . In the instance of
sheep-crossing, Dr. Wells, on the Island of Grenada, had a flock of ewes
served by a ram procured for the purpose. The ewes were *white* and
woolly. The ram was of a chocolate color, and long-*haired* like a goat.
The lambs came much like the male parent. Next year, and afterwards, the Doctor brought a white woolly ram to the island, precisely
of the breed of his ewes. But the lambs continually showed the distinct marks of resemblance, in the *chocolate* color and *hair* of the first
ram — for years afterward — though bred steadily to the white woolly
buck.

Mr. Chas. H. Edmonds, of Melrose, a few years ago, had a fine yard
of Felch's and Burnham's Light Brahmas — among which he allowed
a Seabright cock to run, for a few weeks. I suggested to him my
opinion on what I considered this error, and he sold his Seabrights. In
the fall, his Light Brahma chicks were marked with distinct Golden
Seabright feathers — and for two years succeeding, this marking showed
itself on scores of his chicks, from this very flock of Light Brahmas,
when the Seabright cock had been gone from his premises over two
seasons. But the quagga had been there once, and left his mark, forever, on that Light Brahma stock, and Mr. E. sold them out. . . . . Mr.
Weymouth's experience with Light Brahmas and a brace of Seabright
cocks, which he permitted to travel among the former, was similar. It
took him three seasons to get rid of foul (yellow) feathers in his Light
Brahma pens, after the Seabrights were taken away. . . . . Dr. Simpson,
an eminent physician of Edinburg, states that a young woman, born of
white parents, whose mother, prior to marriage, bore a mulatto child by
a negro man-servant, showed distinct traces of the negro in her short,
curly hair, and pink spots beneath the finger-nails. . . . . Dr. Carpenter
writes, in his latest work on physiology, that it is very common for a
widow who marries again, to bear children most resembling the *first*
husband. . . . . Dr. Harvey affirms that instances are quite frequent,
among the lower animals, where the offspring show, over and beyond
the characteristics of the male by which they were begotten, the
peculiarities of the male by which their mother had *previously* been
impregnated. . . . . The pertinacity with which hereditary traits cling
to the organization in a latent, masked, or undeveloped condition,
long after they might be supposed to be "bred out," is often remark-
able. Breeders of Shorthorn cattle know what is called the "Galloway
alloy." This originated by employing, for only *once*, a *single* bull of a
different breed; but it is now traceable in this modern variety (after
many years breeding), in the frequent developement of the black or
"smutty muzzle," in descendants of this "strain." . . . . Some years
ago, in the Kennebec Valley, there were a few hornless, or polled cat-

tle. Mr. Payne Wingate shot the last of this race (a bull calf), mistaking it, in the dark, for a bear. For over twenty years afterward, *all* his cattle had horns — when suddenly one of his old cows had a calf which grew up without horns; which Mr. Wingate asserts was the exact image of the *first* bull of that breed brought there..... I bred my pure black Newfoundland bitch "Mona" to a dog of the same species — some years since — for nearly a dozen years. When four years old, I crossed her with a large brown curly-haired Russian mastiff. The pups then came of both colors. Subsequently, I bred her *only* to the Newfoundland. But *never*, afterward, did she produce a litter, among which there were not more or less brown curly-haired pups. And this occurred, too, four years after the Russian dog died.

The experience and opinion of H. A. Mansfield, of Waltham, the cautious and skillful breeder of Dark Brahmas, accords precisely with my own. In a note upon this very subject, received from that gentleman only a week or two since, he says: " I have just returned from the West, and have lately read your ' *Secrets in Fowl Breeding.*' You are *right*. I can most heartily endorse what you have therein written about accidental or intentional crossing of pure-bred hens with *any other* variety, and expecting them to breed true afterward. I attribute my own success to the fact that I never keep any fowls on my premises but the Dark Brahmas ; and the worst that can befall my stock (in this respect) would be the possible access to my breeding hens of an inferior cock *of the same variety.* This I guard against by *never* allowing any but my best cocks to come near my hens."

Mr. Mansfield then adds; " A bit of personal experience on this subject comes to my mind, as I write you this. I once bought a fine looking Dark Brahma hen of a man who also bred Light Brahmas. Her form and color were very good, and I mated her to no less a bird than ' Old Waltham,' a superb Dark Brahma cock, as you know. I saved her eggs carefully, and set them. The result was the hatching of sixteen chicks — eight cocks and eight pullets. One pullet was almost *white*, and the entire brood proved worthless — this choice, well-appearing Dark Brahma hen having, unmistakeably, been crossed by the former owner's Light Brahma cock. She was bred from imported stock, but had been ruined, for clean pure breeding, thus carelessly. The hen and chickens were killed and eaten. At that time, this hen was claimed to be ' of the best stock in America.' Since then, I assure you I have been very careful about introducing a strange bird into *my* runs !"

I could go on, almost interminably, with instances of this character, all "truthfully recorded experiments"—which Mr. Felch so accurately declares, in the preface of his book "are of far more value than any *theory*, however forcibly presented ;" although in the body of his book, he also writes that "there can be *no* chance, as the author of " *Secrets in Fowl Breeding* " asserts, for the dam to be contaminated by a chance copulation with a male not of her breed ;" and again, that " there can be *no* contamination of the blood or breeding of the dam, from this cause," etc.

My article is too lengthy, I am aware. But, with this I have begun and finished my controversy with Mr. Felch, on this question. I anticipate what he may argue, however, to wit : that a fowl is not a human being, a horse, a cow, an ass, a dog, a sheep, or a mule. Very well. Has the Almighty ordained one rule for men, and animals, and another for poultry, in this principle of breeding ? I think *not* — indeed!

Still, what of the results with pigeons and fowls, as recorded by Messieurs Botard, Corbie, Mansfield, and by Messrs. Edmonds, Barnes, Weymouth and myself — all based upon actual, repeated, studied, practical experiments with poultry ! Do *these*, too, go for naught against Mr. Felch's speculative theory ?

If so — so be it.

But I conclude with this "assertion," now made for the first time. I practice what I preach. This is my doctrine as set forth in my books, and as I perform it in my poultry-yards. I *know* it to be correct, and I haven't time (at my age) to try the recommendations Mr. F. proposes to amateurs ; which I consider erroneous, and simply encouraging to a recklessness in breeding which, though Mr. F. may *preach* it, he dare not *practice* in his own runs. Or, if he *means* what he says, when he asserts, in his book, that "there can be *no* grounds for belief that a dam, copulating with a sire of a different breed, loses her purity of blood " (as I positively affirm she *does* — in which "assertion" I am backed by Darwin, Bakewell, Surgeon McGillivray, Secretary Goodale, Messieurs Corbie and Botard, Dr. Wells, Dr. Simpson, Mr. Payne Wingate, Dr. Harvey, Mr. Alexander Morrison, the Royal Keeper of the Horse in England, Dr. Carpenter, Messrs. Barnes, Weymouth, Mansfield, Edmonds, and a host of others whom I cannot mention here, for want of space, and confirmed by more than a quarter of a century of actual personal experience), will Mr. Felch venture to test his own theory practically ?

Will he introduce, for one week, or less, say a good, vigorous, thoroughbred *Brown Leghorn* cock to a pen of the lauded *Light Brahma* descendants of " Lady Childs," " Duchess," " Princess," " Vesta," " Lady Mills " (which latter hen, he says, had only one-fourth Burnham blood in her veins !), " Autocrat Belle," " Maud Williams," — or any of these — and, next year, after the Brown Leghorn Cock shall have been slaughtered, and he has steadily bred the same hens to a pure Light Brahma cock for a twelvemonth, give the American poultry fraternity a " truthful record " of the result of this experiment?

I guess *not!* For, his " pure pedigreed " Brahmas thus treated (and he knows this fact as well as I do), would surely throw chickens ringed, streaked and speckled, *then*, and for all succeeding years of their existence, however subsequently mated." . . . . . . This is *my* experience.

TO PRODUCE PRIME SHOW BIRDS.

Fowl fanciers who aim to produce the finest samples for competition in the public exhibition rooms, annually, have in late years made up a large majority of American breeders of the higher grades and varieties of " thoroughbred " poultry.

The cultivation of prime specimens, with this view — sometimes only a trio or a dozen in a place — has been the studious work of skilled amateurs or more experienced fanciers for years in succession also, in this country.

Other advanced breeders have imported good samples of various kinds, with which they have entered the arena of competition, and frequently borne away the palm as breeders or owners of the favored fowls.

In addition to these two classes of winning " fanciers," there have been many larger American poulterers who have shown superior stock of their own raising, which have deservedly won leading prizes for the best in our show rooms, season after season.

But there are " secrets " about raising such successful show-fowls, which *all* who undertake to accomplish this thing have not yet compassed. And some of these " points " we propose to explain, to the best of our ability.

We have cultivated a great many superior fowls in our time ; and in years past we have been very successful in the exhibition-rooms, amongst lively competitors !

We entertain no doubt that most of the fowls imported from China or from Europe — after careful manipulation and domestication under skillful hands in America — are greatly improved upon the originals, in the progeny we produce.

Evidence of this is furnished in the fine *Cochins* among us of various colors, and in the *Brahmas* of late days ; the original stock of all which varieties came from abroad, and which, after being bred in the United States a few years skillfully, have been sent to England and other countries hence, admittedly the finest samples of poultry in the world, as we are all aware.

And this very stock again, first so improved among Americans, has subsequently been farther improved upon in England; and the *progeny* of our own productions here (raised in Great Britian) have once more been returned to us, British-branded, in many an instance still better than those we have supplied the material for in the first place, from American cultivated flocks.

Noting this advance made through careful handling and judicious mating, on both sides of the Atlantic, from year to year — our most ambitious fanciers continue to aim for improvement upon all previous efforts. And it may be safely assumed that, in 1875 and '76, at the principal public American exhibitions there were displayed in quantity and quality the best pens of show-fowls ever seen here, yet — of the leading varieties.

The attainment of this high standard of excellence has been effected only through studious and well-considered experiments in breeding. Certain "strains" of prime stock have been pretty well established, and these have been sought for largely in all quarters, at liberal prices, in consequence of their popularity.

These birds and their progeny, when properly selected and cautiously mated, have produced other good samples which have proved winners, and subsequently fine breeders, of their kind. Yet these very birds that have frequently been named "first" or "second" prize-takers in our shows, amidst strong competition, have disappointed the purchasers of the leading favorites, who have paid round figures for, and attempted to breed them, afterwards. They have been *mated* wrongly in the show-pen, as to color or points, or both; and the buyer of these showy fowls has found that they would neither produce their like, nor were they equal to the production of chickens in many respects so fine as were the "premium" birds, themselves.

This has been occasioned through no fault on the part of the owner, who may have been inexperienced in this nice matter of the proper *mating* of birds for breeding. It certainly was no fault of the purchaser, who was not posted as to this "secret" in chicken-breeding.

Yet the man who publicly shows such superior pairs or trios of fowls in competition now-a-days, or who offers them for sale at extravagant prices for *breeders*, (and which novices in the art take for granted are all right for this purpose) should exercise more discretion in the mating of his stock —*for his own interests in the future*, if for no other reason.

And we do not question that the time is not far distant when well-informed *judges* will be found in our show rooms who will give large consideration to this important point of the proper mating of birds in the exhibition pens, when they award their premiums to "the best" fowls, for breeding purposes.

If we take such an apparently nicely *matched* trio of Light Brahmas, for example, (or any similar parti-colored fowls) *all* having well defined *dark* neck-hackles and saddle feathers, and breed these three together, we shall get from them pullets with black-spotted backs, and still blacker and more distinct dark neck-hackles; while the cocks will grow darker and darker, annually, (from such selections) until they are splashed all over with black patches, from crown to tail-coverts and flanks. And this continuously.

If, on the other hand, we select the dark-hackled pullets, and a *light*-hackled cock for breeding, we get a majority of evenly-marked cocks and nicely "pencilled" neck pullets, in the progeny. Or, if we choose a dark-hackled cock, to place with extreme light-plumed pullets or hens, a similar medium result occurs in the plumage of the chickens bred from this *only proper mode* of mating.

To attempt to breed good even-colored chicks from a clutch of parti-colored fowls *all* light-hued, or *all* dark-plumed, is folly, if we seek to produce the "happy medium" color so

generally desirable. And this mode of attempting the production of future exhibition fowls, even from the beautiful
" first premium " specimens we often so greatly admire in the
show rooms, will invariably prove abortive.

You cannot breed their like from birds of this uniform
extreme color. Yet how common is it, how universal, almost,
to meet with only the dark-necked cock and the clear black
hackled pullets or hens in the same coop, at shows, which are
declared by judges and visitors to be " splendidly *mated?*"

But " matching " is not *mating*, by any means. And it follows thus with all kinds of colored fowls — Brahmas, Games,
Polands, Hamburgs, Plymouth Rocks, Dominiques, Dorkings, Houdans, Bantams, any parti-colored variety. With
the Plymouth Rocks, or the Dark Brahmas, *black* chickens
can largely be produced, if we but select and mate together
of either of these sorts the darkest colored birds we breed,
for two or three years in succession. And all efforts to
obtain even-colored chicks, as a rule, from any combination
except with one sex lighter-plumed than the other, is utterly
futile.

We may otherwise get a few in a hundred that will suit us
perchance. But the other eighty or ninety will be comparatively valueless, in the esteem of the nice breeder.

If they would come light or dark, as a *whole* (in each
chick) this would do. But they do not show either extreme
in feathering ; and in by far the larger part they will be of a
mixed, clouded, patched, or mingled hue — with the white
where the black should prevail, or *vice versa ;* utterly disqual-
ifying either cocks or pullets for any good purpose as breeding-
stock in their future.

But this may be obviated with a little common sense and
fair judgment ; and so time may be saved as well. In every
case where these parti-colored birds are bred, no matter
whose strain they may come out of, be it Burnham's, Felch's,
Plaisted s, Williams', Comey's, or others, and no matter how
fine the parentage appears in the show-room, or in the poultry

papers — in all cases choose for your " matings " one sex of *lighter* plumage and marking than are those of the opposite sex you may make use of.

With colored fowls — like the Cochins, the Leghorns, the Games, the Hamburgs, the Polands, etc., the methods of mating for clean color, of their several varieties, is in no wise different from that to be observed with the Brahmas.

If the union is to be made of black, brown and gold feathering, the birds possessing the medium shades of these colors in the cock or hen, as against the extreme darker tints and markings of either, should be mated together — for average good results.

But it is all experimental, with strange birds. When a breeder knows his strain, and has brought his leading stock up near to perfection, he can tell much more accurately than can the breeder who is not acquainted with a particular variety, or strain, how to go to work to produce generally satisfactory results in feathering, and in other fine points.

It is a study, this. And it cannot be learned in a brief experience. The main secret in reproducing good even-colored pullets, and well plumed cocks, however, lies in mating them strictly as we have now suggested.

Other nice points — such as fine carriage, good size, symmetrical form, well-shaped head, clean comb (of its kind) full leg-feathering on the Brahmas and Cochins, &c., are minor considerations, but of consequence, still, in mating.

By adopting the careful course suggested as to mating for correct plumage, one grand secret will be developed. You may in this way succeed in obtaining a much larger proportion of chicks of the *right* colors you seek, in the right parts of the cocks or hens — and those too that will make the finest show fowls at maturity, by odds — so far as beauty and accuracy of marking is concerned.

But there are other desirable qualities and characteristics to be sought for, as well as good plumage. " Fine feathers make fine birds," it is said. But not *alone*—in domestic fowls.

And we will next consider how we may best unite these other good qualities with that of accurate and correct plumage, so as to render show-fowls the most presentable, and really the most valuable as breeders.

NICE POINTS IN FOWL CULTURE.

THE foregoing explanations of the secrets involved in un-intentional or accidental *crossing* of fowls; as to the probable manner and time when *fertilization* of the egg occurs; of the prime importance of judicious *mating* of the two sexes in breeding to feather; and how prime specimens may best be produced, for *exhibition* stock — are not to be found (within our knowledge) in ordinary poultry books.

Scores of volumes have been printed, in which are set down various " instructions " to the uninitiated, regarding what may happen to the breeder, if this or that elaborate advice be followed.

But the real undercurrents and foundation of the subtle modes through which nature operates, to produce among birds and animals what man admires and aims to imitate, through artificial means, are but slightly appreciated by many breeders, even in our enlightened day.

The old-styled duck-legged " Creeper," or Bakie fowls, of which few are seen now-a-days, were for many years great favorites among our farmers, as layers or sitters. And they were most excellent mothers, too. But it was found, on account of their abbreviated shanks, that they did not make a presentable fowl when dressed, and the longer-limbed barn-yard birds were bred upon this variety to improve the latter; which resulted in giving a more desirable shape to the common poultry of the country.

Now, as to form and symmetry, these must not be neg-lected in poultry bred for prizes — while other standard features and qualities besides accurate plumage must be considered, as well; such as color of legs, shape of comb, carriage, size and weight, condition, etc. And while we are looking to breed feathers nicely, none of these other qualifications must be lost sight of.

The parent-stock should not be too long legged, though a good length of shank in Brahma or Cochin *pullets* I have never found objectionable. The combs and heads of both sexes in the larger kinds are best if small in proportion to the average size of the variety. The carriage of all birds should be upright and sprightly. A dumpy, sluggish, lazy cock, of any breed whatever, isn't worth his feed for reproductive purposes. Even the heavy Cochins and Brahma males should be selected for their vigor and active propensities; and the dull, clumsy, over-grown lunkheads should be cast aside altogether, as breeders.

With the Black Spanish, Hamburgs, Leghorns, Dominiques, etc., there is no difficulty in making desirable selections of males possessing the last mentioned good qualities. Use a medium legged cock, rather than one long or short-legged, then, of the Asiatics, and an average shanked bird of other varieties.

The *color* of the legs is important. With the Cochins and Brahmas, avoid the inclination to flesh-colored shanks. This shows itself, sometimes, upon the otherwise best of birds. But it is highly objectionable, and should never be bred from, when clean yellow legs can be had.

The shape of comb is an important item. This should be accurately formed, and perfect in its way, as nearly as is possible. If it be rose-comb, pea-comb, single-comb, spiked-comb, or whatever belongs to the variety being bred — let this feature be fully and clearly developed. With many of our best show judges, the fine well turned head of a fowl, (especially of the cock), surmounted by a perfect comb of its kind, is a strong recommendation in the bird's favor, to commence with.

Condition next. Now let it be understood that " condition " does not mean fatness, adiposity, corpulency, mammoth size, or enormous weight ; but, literally, condition of general health, apparent stamina, natural strength of habit, and lively unforced exterior, generally.

The " cramming " process has long been in vogue in certain quarters, and some fanciers deem it essential towards putting their fowls for the show room into " good condition " that they must stuff them inordinately — hens and cocks — for a month prior to exhibition days.

No more senseless folly than this was ever indulged in ! A judge in a poultry show who could not discover the results of this foolish trick, ought not to pass upon these Asiatics. Yet the folly is repeated every year.

The fowls are by this unnatural means ruined for future usefulness as breeders — though, (as we have observed in more than one instance) they have gone the rounds of the exhibitions at all points, as show birds. And they have sometimes proved winners — but not always — under intelligent judging.

After these considerations, come the points of size and weight, without reference to extra *fattening*. The standard establishes the limits for excellence in this respect, according to the kind of fowl shown. It has been thought by many American fanciers that great *size* among the Asiatics is a chief recommendation of merit; and to this point most ambitious young breeders give a large share of their attention, in preparing specimens for the show rooms.

But this idea that the " biggest rooster must be the best," is rapidly being educated out of view, among our foremost breeders. And a fifteen-pound cock, or a twelve-pound hen (unless other points of excellence be equal) are not winners against fair full weights in birds that clearly possess other required good qualifications.

The well feathered shanks for Brahmas and Cochins, the " barred " plumage in Plymouth Rocks, the white or creamy ear-lobe in Leghorns, the rose-comb on the Dominiques and

Hamburgs, the "station" and "hardness of feather" in Games, the fifth toe in Dorkings and Houdans, etc., are minor requisites comparatively, perhaps — because these are developments mostly natural to pure-bred birds of these varieties, and as a rule, "take care of themselves." The absence of these distinctive marks evinces a fault in the stock, at once ; and birds deficient in these requisites should never be bred from for exhibition purposes, where "pure" stock is looked for.

And here pertinently comes in a most interesting question, embodying more than one secret of importance — which we will discuss in another chapter.

WHAT IS A PURE-BRED FOWL?

WE reply to this frequently proposed query, first, that an absolutely pure unadulterated specimen of domestic poultry probably does not exist, of any known sort. *All* fowls are made up from the wild originals — and their descendants.

The Eastern varieties, themselves — such as have come out

first and last from Asia, China, the Mediterranean, France, England, etc., of every description — are but the descendants of the early " jungle " races, so far as history informs us.

We have detailed accounts of the Bankiva, Soncrat's, the Ceylon, the Java, the Fire-back, Temminck's, the Australian, etc., imported centuries ago into Europe, and thence to the South, to England, to Italy, to Holland, to France, or Spain — from some of which descended all the present known Games, Cochins, Brahmas, Spanish, Dorkings, Leghorns, Houdans, Polands, Hamburgs, Dominiques, Bantams, etc. And each of the above-mentioned modern styled varieties has been grown, at some period, in a *locality* which gives it its nomenclature.

The Cochins and Brahmas from China, the Black Spanish and Games from Spain the East, or the Mediterranean, the Leghorns from Italy, the Houdans and Creve-cœurs from France, the Hamburgs from Germany or England, the Dominiques from Holland, the Dorkings from Surrey, Eng., or the Bantams from everywhere, (bred down to pigmies from the larger varieties) are thus denominated specifically, because, as far as we know, these modern varieties were generally first established in the countries from which they are thus named.

In every instance cited above, with the single exception of the " *Brahmas* " (which are an American made fowl) these birds are the common domesticated barn-yard variety of the country they hail from. And myriads of them may be found in those countries, in all directions, running about the homesteads of the natives or the country peasants, quite unconscious of their consequence, or their popularity away from their own dung-hills.

Yet *these* are what are designated " pure " breeds. And so they are — when clean bred — as nearly as any fowls *can* be pure. They breed to feather, to size, to general markings, and other specific characteristics. And we call this or

that a " pure Dorking," a " pure Black Spanish," a " pure
Leghorn," a " pure Cochin," or what-not.

Now, what must be admitted as a pure variety of any description, is that which produces its like in both sexes, when
bred together ; and which continues to breed its like, continually, without important deviation from the original parentage,
in color, markings, shape, size, and general features.

All may be, and many are improved by manipulation and judicious handling, through proper selection and mating, from
year to year. But these cannot be *changed* from the original
acknowledged type — in any considerable measure — without
" crossing," or by the infusion of blood foreign to their kind.

And this creates another variety — which, from time to
time, we notice is produced and claimed as "a new breed,"
as in the instances of the " *Brahmas*," the " *Plymouth Rocks*,"
the " *Erminets*," the " *Seabrights*," or our latest beautifully
bred American " *Game Bantams* " of different hues and
strains.

An instance in point, just here we will notice, illustrative
of this theory in connection with " pure " breeds, that we
deem applicable, and which has proved interesting — experi-
mentally — in the experience of some American fanciers.

Nearly thirty years ago, His Royal Highness Prince Albert
of England, sent to Hon. Daniel Webster of Marshfield, a
few " Golden Pheasant " fowls — the first of this beautiful
variety ever seen in the United States — and of a breed
similar to that at present known in this country as " Golden
Spangled Hamburgs." (Not the crested " Golden *Polands*,"
as these others were clean polled.)

Mr. Webster placed this consignment in the hands of Col.
Samuel Jaques, of " Ten Hills Farm," Medford, to breed.
And the Colonel subsequently produced from this pretty
stock many scores of very accurately bred birds, which were
sold in later years all about the country, under the name of
" Golden Pheasant " fowls.

In 1850 to '52, Dr. John C. Bennett, of Plymouth, Mass.,

obtained some of these specimens, and about the same time received a few pairs of the white-crested Black Polish variety. These two he bred together, and the cross gave him *crested* " Golden Pheasants," which he prided himself on, for a time.

Then he attempted, by crossing the *White* Leghorn with a Black white top-knot *Poland*, to produce what he had heard of (but never saw), to wit, a *black*-crested *White* Polish.

He did not succeed in this undertaking, however. He got patched fowls, speckled hens, etc., but the *crest* came mottled or clouded, only; never a clean *black* top-knot, upon a clear white-bodied fowl. This would have been a splendid acquisition indeed, and would be to-day, if any of our fanciers could establish the variety mentioned!

Still later, there came into vogue the crested Golden (and Silver) Polish variety; and finally the muffed or " bearded " varieties — of which an admirable cut of a well bred hen stands at the head of this chapter.

At first we had the plain crested Golden Polish — without the " beard." Then the muff beneath the under mandible cropped out upon the throat. And now we have both muffled (or bearded) and plain — of this variety — which are bred as the fancy may demand ; and both are rightfully designated " pure bred " fowls, because they produce their like with precision and regularity from either kind of stock, and throw no greater proportion of "sports" or imperfect chickens, than do other so-named and established kinds.

Here we have a " pure " breed (though a new one, for *these* particular varieties have been known in America, but a few years) and they came to us from *England*. Why they are called " Polish," is beyond our ken ! Surely they do not hail from Poland — nor did the original " Golden Pheasant " birds ever see that country. They are English fowls, made up by skillful manipulation *there; as* the first similar Prince Albert birds were, and as Sir John made up his famous " Gold and Silver *Seabright* Bantams."

We cite the above instance merely to show how in *this* case an admitted "pure breed" is accepted as such ; and to afford the reader some basis on which to form an opinion as to " what is a pure-bred fowl," in a general way — since most of our modern poultry varieties are similarly " pure bred," and are made up in the countries they come from in a similar way, through skillful handling and judicious mating for points, for color, for markings, for feather, for crests, for muffs, for combs, for fifth toes, etc., etc.

But the limits of this little work do not afford me space to enter more fully into this intricate subject. Yet the secret of what " a pure fowl" is, I have thus touched upon, and will conclude by completing a general answer to the question suggested, as follows ;

No *variety* of animal is strictly " pure," one more than another ; for instance note our fancy rabbits, our various kinds of dogs, or cattle, or sheep, or pigeons. Each comes of and from a given type ; and all are altered in color, length of ears, shape, proportions, plumage, etc., by local circumstances, change of climate, and perpetuation under different surroundings. But *all* descend from distinctive wild originals.

Each variety is produced by artificial selection and breeding, and the term " pure breed " can simply be assumed in a comparative sense — especially as applied to poultry.

A cross between any two or three varieties, gives us a mongrel ; and only mongrels succeed them in the progeny, for years afterwards. The best, the strongest, the most perfect in markings, etc., bred from these, and still annually selected and cautiously mated, will give us nominally "new varieties ; " which in course of time can be brought down to a fine point in general exterior or fixed characteristics, which may warrant their being denominated " a breed."

The " Plymouth Rocks " of to-day are a case in point, and the American Standard accepts them as a distinct established variety of fowl. Yet we all know they are a recent cross, though they are now being bred in this country in many places very nicely, and have proved a "decided hit."

The Light Brahmas we also know come from original Eastern blood, and they have bred wondrously perfect in this country and in England, for twenty-five years. Yet that these parti-colored fowls are a cross of the black and white fowl of China, at some remote early time, there is not a shadow of doubt in the minds of those who know this variety best. And the "Brahmas" of our day are rightfully acknowledged an American production — because they were first recognized in this country, and have from the outset been cultivated at their best, and have been improved and reproduced by thousands, very nearly like the originals, within the United States.

These fowls are as "pure" to-day as are the Dorkings, the Games, the Leghorns, the Houdans, the Cochins, or other modern named variety — and as nearly "thoroughbred."

Yet, like all others, they do not come absolutely uniform in plumage, in comb, in proportions, or in shape. One man breeds what he terms a particular "strain" of this breed. Another has a strain he calls his own. A third reproduces his Brahmas from a family to which he gives a distinctive name, from his early owned sire — as the "Yorkshire Duke," or the great "White Prince," or the big-headed "Autocrat."

And *all* are pure Brahmas; that is to say, as pure as are any well known variety.

And so — as to purity of breed — we should secure the best we can find, of any chosen sorts. When we get them, we must continue to breed them as purely as we receive them. By careful selection afterwards from the progeny, breed only the best, again, of either sex. And thus we may continue to preserve the purity of the "breed" and help to improve the variety, from time to time.

Whatever we do, there will crop out the "sports" and imperfect specimens we so frequently read about, inevitably. These should be disposed of in the shambles, or put into the pot. And if we continue to cultivate only THE BEST, we may readily obtain enough of these in perpetuation to satisfy the most fastidious taste as to their general " purity," and be able to supply the liveliest demand in the future.

The amalgamation of the improved Light Brahmas of different strains — or the breeding of the Felch, the Burnham, the Tees, the Williams, the Comey, the Plaisted, the Todd, or the Buzzell strains, one with the other — has been largely resorted to in all directions, of late years, by fanciers.

It matters very little which of these favorites are chosen to operate with, so that good, sound, well-pointed, clear-colored, fair sized, vigorous specimens be obtained. Any of them are good enough — when you can procure the better class of samples ; and all these gentlemen have earned a goodly reputation for their average productions.

So it is with other varieties. There are half a dozen strains of good White and Brown Leghorns, of prime Gold and Silver Hamburgs, of excellent Games,* of thoroughbred Cochins, of admirable Dorkings and Dominiques, of beautiful Bantams, etc., etc., now popular in this country. But none are better than the others — when they are clean bred, and carefully manipulated.

PREPARING BIRDS FOR EXHIBITION.

There are legitimate means for preparing fowls for the exhibition-rooms, which most contributors to these entertaining annual gatherings have never made themselves acquainted with — but which are practiced in England with success, and which some few American fanciers have in late years adopted, to similar advantage.

---

* The *Game* varieties we have said but little about in this work ; as in PART THREE (published in a volume by itself, following this present treatise), we devote the contents *exclusively* to that widely disseminated and generally esteemed breed. See announcement at close of this volume.

Amongst the modes in vogue, where the matter is under-stood — that of especial *feeding*, for the three or four weeks preceding the show, is not uncommon. If this be judiciously done, no ultimate harm comes to the fowls thus treated — though they are not subsequently much benefitted, by this process, be it premised.

A diet of barley and buckwheat daily, for a single feed, in the morning; a second meal at noon of vegetables and rice or Indian corn meal, boiled in milk; and a full evening feed of whole wheat and sound corn, will make a wondrous difference in a bird's "condition" in twenty days' time — after ordinary feeding.

If to the above regimen you add a dry feed of sunflower-seed and hemp-seed, between the noon and evening meals, it will prove highly advantageous towards glossing the plumage, and heightening the color of comb and wattles, for the time being.

All this is artificial, be it understood, and its effects are transitory. Very little green food should be allowed, during this extra feasting. The oily nature of the seeds will act as a sufficient laxative, for all present purposes. The meaty properties of the grains mentioned will help the birds to flesh up fully, without creating over-much of internal fat. And after the exhibitions are over, they can be placed upon ordinary rations, or even "short commons," for a week or two; when they will resume their normal condition, without experiencing great discomfort or noticeable injury, if you do not *cram* them in this process.

Another plan in use across the water is the careful *washing* of the show-fowls, the last thing before they are sent to the exhibitions. This is a simple performance, when properly done, and cleanses the plumage of white or light colored birds from all stains and outward blemish, for the nonce. It is done by rubbing clean white or transparent soap through their first dampened feathers, and then with a stiff brush dipped in clear water removing the soap, by moving it briskly downward and backward from neck to rump, until no suds is perceptible from the action.

When the plumage is dry, a second careful brushing, or combing, will smooth all out nicely, and the bird is thus rendered outwardly more presentable.

But the alkali in the soap, although cleansing, will dim the natural lustre of the feathering, unless it is all cleaned out thoroughly, at the end of this procedure. When well done, this is a good method. If but half done, it is worse than nothing.

After this plumage-bath is concluded, saturate a bit of sponge in a concoction of alcohol and olive oil, (well mixed) and bathe the comb, wattles, shanks and feet with it. Then rub these parts off clean, and the fowl will look fresh, healthy and bright, from beak to toes, This last process should be performed on the day prior to sending the birds to the show rooms.

An easier plan to render the plumage glossy and bright at this brief forcing term, is to place the fowls intended for exhibition purposes for a fortnight previously in a roomy covered pen, with broadside to the sunlight, and strew the floor with clean short-cut new rye-straw, six or eight inches in depth — where they should be kept away from the earth.

Cocks and hens, during this preparation, should not be enclosed *together ;* nor should they ever be shown in exhibition-coops without an open fixed parting between the sexes, in their cages. Thus their nice plumage remains unruffled, and they appear at their best — in December or January.

Fresh water daily, and plenty of clean dry sand (not ashes) to roll in, in their straw-bedded coops, will help to keep them healthy and flourishing.

When the exhibitions are over, let the hens come to the fresh soil again, as soon as possible. Put them upon ordinary good diet, with the cocks, and they will do well again.

The recommendations embodied in this chapter are all admissible and proper. Every one desires to " put his best

foot foremost " at the exhibitions. And any extra effort to
place the show stock in its most attractive possible trim, is
perfectly advisable, and laudable.

It will be found that most of the Asiatic varieties are very
persistent in the desire to set, if we attempt to thwart them
in their purpose. I have therefore found it far the best way
to *allow them to sit for a couple of weeks,* on glass or wooden
eggs. Then remove them, *at night,* and place them upon the
roosts.

Break up their nest, and displace it, next morning. They
will rarely give you trouble after this. If they do — put them
upon the grass, in a floorless open coop, for a day or two, in
company with a young rooster. They will shortly go to laying
again. And having had two weeks' rest and quiet, the
"broody" fever will have passed away.

This is the easiest way to "break them up," and it requires
less time to do it *surely,* than is usually lost in the various
inhuman modes adopted by novices for this purpose.

NOTABLE AMERICAN "STRAINS."

WE devote a few pages to what have become known in this
country as American "strains" of well-bred fowls.

It may be well to state at this point, that the word *strain*
signifies simply a favorite family, or ancestry. Duchess
short-horn cattle are called the "Duchess strain." Sheep,
from Mr. Bakewell having established this distinct variety,
are known as the "Bakewell strain." The Game fowl, as
bred on the Earl of Derby's estate, was known as the
"Derby" strain. Some American poultry-breeders claim a
"strain" title for certain favorite *fowls* — such as have come
down from the "Autocrat," the "Duke of York," "Colossus,"
the "White Prince" strain, etc.

We shall here mention the "Light Brahmas" first, because

this is our own original favorite, as is now pretty well known, the world over.

There has seemed to exist a deal of secrecy about the origin of this famous breed, but it really comes from Chinese stock —the very *first* birds of this kind ever seen having been shown by the author in 1849 and '50. This stock has been largely bred, in all sections, and certain ambitious breeders since 1853 and '54 have given exclusive attention to multiplying this favorite race, and successfully.

In 1852, I sent to the Queen of England a cage of these fowls, then a year old, bred in my yards at Melrose. Portraits of these mature birds (then called "Grey Shanghaes") were published in leading poultry books and papers, both in the United States and in England, as were also those of the progeny, one and two years old, in 1850, '51, '52 and '53. This settles the point as to precedence in date of origin, and period of early breeding.

Mr. Plaisted began in 1853 to breed the *now* so-called "Light Brahmas." And since then he has at times produced some very good specimens. In 1874 and '75 he bred what he called the "Knox-Chamberlain strain," (whatever that may be), about which I know nothing, and never heard of, until Mr. P. wrote something about it, in the year 1874.

Mr. E. C. Comey, of Quincy, has for some years bred a strain out of his famous "Duke of York" and "Autocrat" birds that have proved remarkably fine ; and which have had a wide distribution all over the country. Mr. Comey has raised from these, and their descendants, hundreds of first-class cocks and hens, which have proved subsequent winners at our American shows.*

A later breeder (in point of time) by a few years, is Mr.

* Mr. I. K. Felch in his recently published "Manual," says that this "*Duke of York*" and "*Autocrat*" both came from eggs laid by the Phillips hens—and Mr. Phillips just before he died, informed Mr. E. C. Comey that he procured his fine Light Brahmas from G. P. Burnham's stock ; the same as that sent by Mr. B. to Queen Victoria. Mr. Comey had previously stated this same fact to us, personally.

G. P. B.

I. K. Felch, of Natick. He commenced with a cock of the Light Brahma variety, which he bought for a dollar or two in the street, from a market-man's wagon. And with a few good hens, said to be of the Cornish-Chamberlin stock, he subsequently produced a strain which he calls his own — that breed the pea-comb almost invariably, and have proved very superior as a general thing — because he has taken great pains in their culture; and through wise selections from his own and other fine strains which he has judiciously mated, until at the present time the Felch stock is as well known and as highly esteemed, for its general good quality, as any in the United States.

Mr. Philander Williams of Taunton, has produced and exhibited in the last ten years many first-class *Light* and *Dark* Brahmas, and few breeders in this country have been more fortunate, or have so well sustained their good repute, as has Mr. Williams.

And scores of other fanciers who have been engaged in this speciality for a less term of years than those above alluded to, have contributed their quota towards improving this fine species.

In every instance where a notable success has followed their efforts, the work of these breeders has been persistent and earnest toward the object in view. In this way *only* can success be attained. From the outset these men procured the best stock birds they could find, from whatever source, and what they esteemed the purest in blood. They bred these selections with care, and zeal, and good judgment. They mated their stock judiciously, and watched critically for results. As changes became necessary, they changed their breeders, and infused new blood into those they had experimented with previously, perhaps less satisfactorily.

And finally they have brought to a goodly state of perfection what they call their own strains — until we now hear constantly of the merits of the Felch, the Plaisted, the Weymouth, the Williams, the Comey, the Todd, the Dibble, the Buzzell, or other "strain," which has deservedly its host of admirers.

In a similar way the Partridge Cochins have been perfected by such fanciers as W. H. Bracket of Boston, and C. H. Bradley of Conn., as well as the White Leghorns of Mr. Pitkin of Hartford, and J. Boardman Smith of North Haven, Conn., or the Brown Leghorns of Messrs. Kinney and Bonney of Mass., Mr. Ongley's elegant Spangled Hamburgs, the beautiful Pea-comb Partridge Cochins of C. H. Edmonds of Melrose, the choice Dark Brahmas of H. A. Mansfield at Waltham, the Plymouth Rocks, of F. H. Corbin, Newington, and others in Connecticut; and scores of producers of other varieties; none of whom have made themselves eminent save through careful, consistent, devoted effort in the right direction, continually, in the production of their favorite and popular kinds of choice poultry, at present so well known the country over.

We might mention many other notable instances of first-class breeding from what is popularly called original "pure" stock; but lack of space here prevents extending the reference. We quote these fanciers because they lead the van, on this side of the Atlantic.

They have acquired some of the main "secrets in fowl-breeding" through a love of their occupation, and by active intelligence and constant devotion to the pleasant work. Through such means alone can we any of us similarly succeed in this peculiar enterprise.

BRIEF ADVICE TO SELLERS AND BUYERS.

Here we conclude our second treatise, which is offered as a companion volume to our recently published "*Diseases of Domestic Poultry*," in uniform style with this, by suggesting the following brief advice to the seller and the buyer of any variety or strain they may propagate, or desire to experiment with.

Go to head-quarters for these fancy birds, always — and pay fairly for what you desire, when you seek "the best" fowls to be had. Never aim to cheapen the stock you may choose. *Good* birds, of all the best sorts, command leading prices, invariably; and these higher qualities cannot be produced in *all* of the fowls that even a careful fancier may cultivate — on the average.

Buy such birds from breeders of repute, who have too much at stake to cheat you. No man who charges you the higher figures demanded for a pair or trio of the better sorts now-a-days, can afford to raise them to maturity, for merely market poultry rates. And when he sells at his own price, he can much less afford to send you poor birds — for this unwise and unjust course would quickly destroy his hard-earned reputation.

The fortunate seller who may have reached that position where the public have confidence in his ability to produce such desirable stock, and who steadily practices the precepts of the golden rule, will always find *this* mode of dealing with novices, amateurs, or others, the only true system whereby he may continue on successfully in the fancy chicken trade.

This final suggestion is one of the "secrets in fowl breeding" that it takes some years of experience to learn! But, though the last we shall now mention, it is by no means the *least* worthy of every honorable dealer's careful consideration.

———

THE third volume is now published of same size and form, and is devoted to *Games*, exclusively.

This is handsomely illustrated with specimens of the finest varieties of this gallant race of poultry known in America; and contains concise directions for the mating, feeding, handling, breeding, heeling and matching of these popular birds; together with practical advice as to the curing of their especial diseases, wounds and ailments.

This last mentioned work, published in March, 1877, will be found complete in its way. It will be appreciated by the large class of GAME breeders in the United States, who will find this little book very nicely got up, and well worth its moderate cost to any and every fancier in the country who is interested in breeding this immensely favorite class — the foremost of domestic fowls — and for variety, what is universally conceded to be "the noblest Roman of them all."